CROSSING THE BOUNDARY

Black Women Survive Incest

Melba Wilson

SEAL PRESS

Library of Congress Cataloging-in-Publication Data

Wilson, Melba.

Crossing the Boundary : Black Women Survive Incest

p. cm.

Originally published: London : Virago Press Ltd., 1993.

Includes bibliographical references and index.

ISBN 1-878067-42-7 : $12.95

1. Incest—United States. 2. Incest victims—Psychology. 3. Adult child sexual abuse victims—Psychology. 4. Afro-American women—Psychology. I. Title.

HQ72.U53W5 1994

306.877—dc20

93-4813

CIP

First published by Virago Press, 1993

First Seal Press edition, March 1994

10 9 8 7 6 5 4 3 2 1

Distributed to the trade by Publishers Group West

Dedicated to those of us who survived,
and to those of us who didn't

CONTENTS

ACKNOWLEDGEMENTS

While in one way writing this book has been a very solitary experience at times, in quite another, it has involved the love and support of a great number of people, who have lived with me and with my ups and downs in working on it over the past three years. In that sense, it has been very much a communal experience.

Although they know who they are, it is important that you, too, know who they are, because they were an indispensable part of the process that allowed this book to come to fruition.

I must, first of all, thank the women who allowed me into their homes and into their confidences concerning their experiences of incest, and who asked only that I tell our stories.

For their early help during my researching of the book, I also thank Marlene Bogle, Pat Agana, Liz Kelly and Anne Clark. My sincerest thanks must also go to Olive Gallimore and Juliette Jarrett, for listening and supporting from that first idea through to reading and commenting on the first draft. To Joyce Hooks must go special thanks for good advice and invaluable comment when I needed it most. Many thanks also to Anne Reyersbach and Joan O'Pray, whose comments from a different perspective allowed me to focus more clearly on my own.

I feel very lucky to have had, as my editor at Virago, Ruth Petrie, to guide me through this first book. Her quiet though unflinching encouragement was a mainstay for me in its preparation.

No acknowledgement would be complete without expressing my heartfelt appreciation to my husband, Jake, for his support, love, encouragement and patience, which was always there, and always has been.

Finally, I must once again pay homage to my grandmother, Lucille Irene Boyd, whose strength and determination imparted to me at an early age the important knowledge that anything was possible, as long as you believed you could do it.

Grateful acknowledgement is made to Random House, Inc. and Virago Press for kind permission to use the extract from Maya Angelou's *I Know Why the Caged Bird Sings* © Maya Angelou 1969; to Michele Wallace for kind permission to use material from *Black Macho and the Myth of the Superwoman*, Verso/MLB, London and New York, 1979, 1990, pp. 89–90 and 106–7 in 1979 edition; to Pat Agana and Urban Fox Press for kind permission to use extracts by Pat Agana © Pat Agana and Urban Fox Press UK, first published in *Passion: Discourses on Blackwomen's Creativity*, 1990, edited by Maud Sulter; to Fontana, an imprint of HarperCollins Publishers Ltd., for kind permission to use extracts from *Bake-Face and other Guava Stories* by Opal Palmer Adisa, 1989.

PREFACE
TO THE U.S. EDITION

This American edition of *Crossing the Boundary* represents an important milestone for me. Firstly, because, being American, and writing from an experience which reflects that fact, I feel the thoughts I have set out ought to be available to those with whom I share home ground. Secondly, I also strongly feel that if there is to be a discussion of incest in black communities, it must be placed on people's agendas, situated into their consciousness. *Crossing the Boundary* is an attempt to begin this process.

The book has received a favourable reception since its English publication, particularly among black people (men and women). In talking with people about their impressions of the book and its subject matter, I have been cheered to find that they seem to be taking from it what I had intended. That is, to view it not just in terms of my story or any one woman's story, but to look at the wider implications of what incest and the continuing silence about its does and has done to us as black people.

I wrote the book for black people, first and foremost. I am speaking directly, in it, to black women and black men. I did not consider very much what its impact might be in the wider community. I have found, however, that what it has to say has been embraced by many: in particular, a number of white women survivors of child sexual abuse have said they found it useful. That is all to the good.

I hope the book will travel well. The Children Act, referred to in Chapter One and elsewhere is, I think, the only area which needs explanation for American readers. The Act became law in England and Wales in 1989, and is intended to safeguard the rights of children and to stress the responsibilities which in the first instance parents, followed by health and/or local authorities (e.g., through social services departments) have towards safeguarding the welfare of children in need. The Children Act, for example, calls for children's wishes and feelings to be taken into account "when a court is determining any question in respect to a child's upbringing."* This has been used with effect, in some cases where children wished to "divorce" their parents.

The Resources section has been changed to reflect an American context. My criteria in compiling the British resources section was to find groups/therapists/organisations which specifically addressed the needs of black women. In this edition, as well, I have tried to include what I think may be useful avenues for black women to explore in order to seek any help they may need. Readers' responses, either regarding the usefulness of those groups and individuals which are listed at the back of the book, or in providing the names of others, would be welcome.

Melba Wilson
October 1993

* The Care of Children, Principles and Practice in Regulations and Guidance, The Children Act, 1989, London, Her Majesty's Stationery Office (HMSO).

INTRODUCTION

I am an incest survivor. Let me qualify that – I am black, female and approaching middle age. I have reached a point in my life where I feel that sharing that information may be useful for those who are also black, female and have survived child sexual abuse. My aim is that it will aid in my own coming to terms with the sexual relationship which occurred more than thirty years ago between my father and me; and help other black women who have similar experiences to be able to do the same.

The fear that I have about saying this publicly is considerable. I worry that this book will be misconstrued and misinterpreted by many in our black communities. Some may feel that I have breached an even greater taboo, crossed a bigger boundary (in their eyes) than incest. By airing publicly some of the uncool stuff that goes on in our communities, I and the other women whose stories are included are exposing the dirty linen that we all know and keep quiet about. Except in rare circumstances (for example, especially brutal occurrences of child sexual abuse (CSA)) tacit approval is given to keeping incest in black communities under wraps.

In common with many black women who have been sexually abused, however, I feel that insufficient import has been given to this most taboo of subjects amongst us. This leaves those of us whom it directly affects wondering what we're supposed to do with the baggage we carry around with us as a result. Any trepidation I have about airing this issue, therefore, is outweighed by my genuine belief that the act of saying it publicly will make it easier for other black women either to admit any abuse they may have suffered and buried, to themselves, or to tell someone else. Second, having maintained a silence about my incest for many years, I know there are very many others within our communities who are doing the same. Furthermore, there seems to be no concerted push to do something about it, either by helping black women survivors to speak about it or, once they do, to tackle it in a straightforward manner. (I do not suggest that no voices are heard speaking out against incest – many of them are included here. Some work is going on – prevention, therapy. It is carried out in pockets, and a lot of it done by survivors and therapists in the field, who are attempting to change the status quo.)

This is a book that I have long wanted to write, though I have not always known that I would or, indeed, even could write it. I do know that I have seldom seen my story as a black woman survivor of incest being told among the many pages that have been written on the subject, and I took that as my guiding impetus for embarking on this project and seeing it through to the end.

I have tried to make it personal and political. I have tried to include much in this attempt at crossing the boundary from silence to giving a voice to black women survivors of incest and CSA. In one sense it is our stories, because we don't often get to hear each other's stories. It's important because once you hear them it's harder to run away from them and pretend they don't exist.

At the same time I feel it's important to do more than just tell our stories. As important as they are, they are not the whole story. The framework of the book is arranged to take account of the influences which led to our abuse in the first place. It is important to explore the mythology about black women's sexuality, for example, in order to fully appreciate the implications of incest in black communities. Likewise, as a black feminist, it was crucial for me to bring to bear that perspective, which informs my life as well as my survival.

A feminist understanding of incest and CSA necessitates looking at roles ascribed to black women, gender- and race-defined stereotypes assigned to black women and black men, and the consequences these have for how we relate politically, socially and sexually.

The aim of the book, too, is to move beyond our abuse. I have discussed ways in which this is helped as well as hindered by, for example, some professional hijacking of survivors and their experiences. My hope is that professionals who misappropriate those experiences will find something contained within the book that will better inform their practices in their work with black women survivors of incest. In addition, I have attempted to show how we can positively move beyond our experiences – not forget, but move on from them. This we can do through therapies which are sympathetic to our needs as black women, and which we ourselves can control.

One of the most crucial aspects for me in structuring what I would say concerned the chapter I have entitled 'Love, comfort and abuse'. It deals with the nitty-gritty of what many survivors carry around with them. Guilt. Guilt which is almost too painful to face. Some of us may feel guilt because we derived pleasure from our abuse; or we may feel guilt because we didn't prevent it. We may even feel guilt because we think our bodies were somehow responsible.

One thing I do want to get across in this book, maybe more than any other, is that it's time we let go of the guilt. It's time we placed it back where it belongs – on those who did not hold their boundaries and chose to sexually abuse the little girls we were. Before we can unburden ourselves of this collective guilt, though, it's important to look at what makes us feel this way. This particular chapter was very hard for me to write because it meant that I had to examine my own guilt feelings, and their effect on my life.

As a consequence of all of this, I knew there were some things that had to be discussed primarily in terms of what incest has meant for me as a black woman, who grew into womanhood carrying a burdensome secret. A secret which I was convinced no other little girl in the world shared. I knew I had to put down all those painful, hurtful, frightful thoughts and feelings that had been buzzing around in my head for years, and that needed to be written down and shared with the many, many others in a position similar to mine.

I write primarily for all those other young black girls out there who grew into womanhood with their own heavy secrets; thinking they, too, were the only ones. I write, also, for their grown-up counterparts who still carry that misused and abused little girl within them, because there was nowhere else for her to go.

I write for Pauline, a young black woman, who was 24 when we met at a conference for black women survivors of child sexual abuse, where I came out publicly as a survivor for the first time. Pauline was in the early stages of recovery from a breakdown. When we met, she was desperately trying to make sense of her abuse and to come to terms with it. She was angry, hurt and bewildered about why it had to happen to her. She felt her mother knew about the incest with her stepfather and with the other men who lived in the rooming-house where she grew up. She believed that her mother had probably even prostituted her.

I write, too, for all those young black girls (and boys) who have not yet made it to adulthood, who are still being abused, and who may even recognise it as abuse (this being 1993); but who are equally trapped within their walls of silence because of unwritten, spoken and unspoken taboos about what should or should not happen; what should or should not be said about what does or does not happen in our communities of colour.

I write for one of my beautiful nieces, who, I discovered in the course of writing this book, was savagely raped by a male relative whom she loved and trusted; and who, because of her mental state, still doesn't know what happened to her.

CHAPTER 1

Myths, realities and matriarchy

Myths

Part of the territory which goes with being black and female is that of contending or being confronted, from time to time, with other people's, often wrong, ideas of who we are as black women. We have been particularly plagued by the stereotype of myth, because historically we have tended to be invisible.

In literature, in politics, in everyday life, it is black women, primarily, who have been responsible for breaking that invisibility. Black male writers ignored or stereotyped us. White writers – male and female – either forgot us or stereotyped us. The women's movement tried to make us over to fit their images of feminism more closely.

Myths abound in relation to black women and sexual abuse – we either wanted it, or we can handle it or we are educated by it. In this particular context such myths are, at best inexcusable, and at worst detrimental to our well-being as women and as survivors. In an effort to understand the harm and/or importance that myth-making has in relation to black women who have been victimised through incest, it is necessary to explore some of those myths as they impact on us as black women and black people. Racism, sexism and perceptions about black women's sexuality play an important part in the perpetration of these myths. It is important to name these myths, discard them and move on.

Myth no 1: Incest is normal in black communities

Black women who survive incest and other forms of child sexual abuse are caught up in a curious anomaly. On the one hand, it is not supposed to exist in our communities, to any degree (or so they say). This brings about a reluctance to raise it as an issue. On the other hand, those of us to whom it's happened and those who perpetrate it, and those who turn a blind eye, *know* it exists – exists to such an extent that it's almost considered normal by many inside and outside black communities.

The widely held perception that it is normal practice in black communities for little black girls to be sexually manhandled by their fathers, grandfathers, uncles, and friends of the family is one of the most damaging myths with which survivors have to contend. Not least because there appears to be little inclination or interest in changing this unhealthy state of affairs. Marlene Bogle, a black woman who has pioneered work as a sexual abuse counsellor in London with black women put it this way:

> Books that have been written on the subject have ignored and excluded any experiences of what it means to be a black survivor. All the myths, stereotypes and racism that surrounds child sexual abuse has portrayed incest as problematic only for white women and children. Black women did not have a place in this, because of the racism inherent in explanations of child sexual abuse. Incest has been seen and believed to be the norm within the black culture and way of life. This is not true. Black women and children do not expect to be sexually abused as a normal part of life. To dismiss this myth, one has to be factual and say that child sexual abuse does not know race, class and creed. It is an international issue that affects us all.[1]

It is curious, though, that while there is such widespread belief that sexual abuse occurs in black communities, one is not aware of an attendant interest in tackling this illegal and inappropriate behaviour in these communities. Information and analysis about the position of the sexually abused child who is black and female is noticeable by its absence in current research. Though numerous studies, reports and articles have been advanced in the field generally, few of these have concentrated on ethnicity and/or culture.

In 1984 two American researchers Pierce and Pierce, in an article outlining race as a factor in CSA, found 'no significant attempt to examine the link between ethnicity and the sexual abuse of children'. They said: 'Moreover, treatment has been approached from a "color-blind" perspective in spite of the suggestion that people of color – specifically blacks – differ from whites in their approach to sexuality.'[2]

This has meant that, as a consequence, incest and child sexual abuse in non-white communities has largely come to be ignored – as an issue to be dealt with either inside or outside those communities; or as a focus for research. Diana Russell, who has carried out one of the few pieces of research concentrating on black women survivors of child sexual abuse has written:

> That the experiences of White victims are assumed to be the norm for all minority victims is evident in the lack of ethnicity-based child sexual abuse research. But the assumption that data on Whites accurately reflect the experiences of the members of all other groups denies the role of cultural differences in people's lives, denies the fact that racism has an impact, and reflects the White bias of most researchers in this field.[3]

I do not claim to be an expert on incest. What I can lay claim to is an ability to empathise with those for whom I write. An empathy so deeply felt that it became important for me to expose myself in this way in order to be able to say to others that as survivors, we owe it to each other not to remain silent any longer. It is not up to us to continue to protect our communities in this way – to pretend that incest and sexual abuse do not occur within them, at the expense of our own well-being. Rather, it is up to our communities to provide the space, the opening for us to come forward, easily and without fear of condemnation, which allows the healing process to begin.

We *must* share our stories, to establish a dialogue about sexual abuse in our families and our communities so that people do not continue to hold to preconceptions and misconceptions about what goes on within them. That is something which is slowly being recognised and taken up by black women survivors of incest and child sexual abuse – most notably, LaToya Jackson, Oprah Winfrey, and writer Carolivia Herron, whose recent novel, *Thereafter Johnnie* (Virago 1992) tackles the subject of incest in a middle-class African-American family. Along with these very public survivors of incest, there is a growing number of other, more anonymous black women survivors who are also taking the decision to come out. Between us we can turn the tide away from silence and acquiescence and towards openness and dialogue.

Incest, though common, is not the norm in our communities. From all that I have been able to find out, it occurs about as commonly in black communities as it does in all other cultures and communities. But we do not talk about it. In part, because we don't really know how to and in part because we learn from an early age that we're not supposed to 'put our business out in the street'. As a black woman who has grown up in the shadow of racism, I am well aware of the costs of letting our defences down in terms of white people taking advantage of weaknesses which may become apparent as a result. But the only recourse to keeping the community's defences up by keeping our mouths shut about the abuse that we know occurs is to suffer an even greater defencelessness that will eventually poison the roots and branches of the tree we're trying to protect.

Myth no 2: Black women can handle it

> The real strength of black women has been mythicized [*sic*]. If a woman has internalized the myth she will feel that 'this is my cross to bear. I'm going to shove it under the rug.' For the black woman the myth of her strength becomes another burden, another oppression that may be internalized.[4]

My starting point is that if we do not discuss the hurt, pain, confusion, guilt and anger and memories of violence that many black women incest survivors carry with them from the time their bodies are victimised, it cannot be assuaged or laid to rest. Long after the dialogue about incest and child sexual abuse began and became established in white communities, it is still not accepted as a concern in our communities. 'That's a white folks problem.'

The predominantly accepted view in black communities is that black women are strong and can handle anything that life throws at them – whether rape at the hands of white slaveowners; the trauma of being separated from their children in slavery; racism; violence against us within our communities, or sexual abuse. About incest and sexual abuse, the entrenched view is that we can and do put it behind us as a tolerable (or at least tolerated) part of our lives, and go on to lead successful lives in spite of it; some would even argue, because of it.

Black women are indeed strong, and I will discuss this more fully in a later chapter. But, despite the popular notion, we are not the 'mules of the world'. We do not possess an interminable ability to take all the shit that may be thrown our way. We can take a lot of it, and we do. But that does not mean to say we enjoy it or wish such a state to continue unchecked. It's about time we made clearer our need for space in which to be vulnerable. The failure to acknowledge the issues raised by incest and other forms of child sexual abuse in our communities, in any kind of reasoned and compassionate way, means that this more damaging of myths continues to oppress us. As a result, many, many black women still carry around with them huge 'mountains' of trauma, because there is nowhere else to place it. If we listen to what black women survivors of incest say about what the pain and trauma of the incest means to them, it becomes impossible to continue to collude in this particular myth:

> I never told anyone – not even my favourite teacher at school. Mostly out of fear that my telling would bring the same results as when I first tried to tell my mother – I was about five years old.
>
> I remember that evening well, and the lesson that I learnt from it – never to tell a soul. I can never forget the look on my mother's face as she hit and kicked and punched me – her anger at me for what I'd said, not at him for what he'd done. I don't remember the words, only the pain as she threw me from one side of the room to the other. And then stood by as my father did the same. And the confusion that reigned in my head. I thought it was my fault, I must have done something wrong. For years after that I tried to hide away from the knowledge that I had been sexually abused as a child.

And many years later:

> One day, though I don't quite know how, I dragged myself along to an 'Incest Survivors Group' meeting. It helped in a small way, in terms of my coming to terms with things. But most of the women were white and that wasn't what I needed. I needed to talk to Black women about it, I needed a safe space. Like I said, outwardly I was accepting the facts, but inwardly I felt an overwhelming need to be with my own kind and talk about my troubles.

> I began to work with two other women to organise a one day workshop for Black Women Survivors of Child Sexual Abuse. About 15 women turned up that day and spent time with each other just acknowledging that we exist. Some of us talked for the first time, some of us didn't talk at all. It was a start. That day gave me strength and sanity. I'd found what I needed at last.[5]

Linda Hollies, an African-American in her forties, was sexually abused by her father throughout her childhood. She describes the incest as 'a mountain that did not have a name or a face' which had impeded her since the age of 12. She writes:

> My father brought this mountain into my world, for you see, I am the victim of incest . . . My father was the assistant pastor of the small, family-type Pentecostal church I was raised in and where God's love was constantly preached: respect for parents was another favorite topic. But the most popular theme was the sinner and the sinner's abode in hell. Well, I had problems. I could not love this man who came into my bedroom and did unmentionable things to me; I could not believe that God could love me and yet allow this to continue. I surely had no respect for my father as a parent. Therefore, I was a sinner, right?
>
> After the break-up of my first marriage, I was a single parent, a working adult and enjoying a measure of success, yet the mountain [of undergoing the trauma of incest] was still in control. My sense of worth was steadily diminishing; nothing covered my deep sense of shame. The 'filth' of my secret was eating me up and there was no one to confide in.[6]

One survivor I spoke to described her particular trauma:

> For a long time I didn't want to have children because I didn't want them anywhere near him [her father]. I didn't want a child who would ask about their grandfather . . . I've started speaking out. I feel that If I don't talk about it I'm denying myself. I've lived with it all along. I'm not going

> to deny it happened to protect the fact that it was done by a brother.

A young Anglo-Asian woman in Britain related her feelings:

> It's just not talked about. Now that I've told, I'm an Untouchable . . . Not many people want to marry into a family where it's gone on . . . I'm getting by and I'm surviving, but there's never a day that goes by you don't think about what happened.[7]

Myth no 3: Incest is a sexual education

Another myth in our communities views sexual abuse and incest as the 'schooling' of young black girls about matters which are sexual. This view no doubt gained ground during slavery when, according to psychologist Beryl Gilroy, who has worked extensively with women survivors from the Caribbean and Africa, black fathers historically performed an 'opening up' of their daughters. As the words imply, the fathers literally sexually opened them up, in preference to allowing an overseer or slavemaster do it. Those historical fathers have their modern-day equivalent, as the following testimony of one survivor bears out:

> When I was 16, I remember coming home from school one day and my mother accusing me of seeing a boy. Dad was no longer abusing me. He used to make me watch him masturbate, though, with a bible in one hand and his penis in the other. I can remember on the eve of my 16th birthday going to bed with a knife. I had this fantasy of not just killing him but of cutting him up into little pieces, because he used to say that he would 'christen' me first.

Some men do, indeed regard the incest as a way of 'christening' or teaching their daughters about sex. Beryl Gilroy notes that some men see it as aiding their daughter's rite of passage into womanhood; and because of this, feel no remorse for the act. For some, it is bound up with the idea of nurturing their daughters. For these men there is a sense of frustration that female ways of nurturing, the breast, for example, are denied them. The next best thing is to introduce their daughters to womanhood via the only way they feel they can – their penis. According to Gilroy, this involves men separating nurturing from culture, for culture imposes taboos which nature does not.

Oftentimes, sleeping arrangements in black families – the close proximity of bedrooms – leads to a lack of restraint. Sometimes, somehow this contributes to a feeling that it can't be sinful or wrong. On the contrary, it may feel natural to the man perpetrating the incest. Natural in the sense that this is an available girl child, and natural in the sense that who better to aid her in her sexual exploration and thus set her firmly on the road to womanhood than a loving father? (This theme will be explored in a later chapter.)

Myth no 4: Black girls/women are sexual animals

Black girls and women are highly sexed, and often promiscuous, says this myth – so why make a fuss about their daddies breaking them in early, I mean, it's better to keep it all in the family, right? My answer to that is: only if you view the family as a place for fostering neuroses and inflicting pain. There are those who will say they cannot see what all the fuss is about. One woman at an international black women's conference noted that 'in the Caribbean child sexual abuse is not recognised as a crime. People will laugh at you if you try to report it.'[8] This view is also reinforced by media images of black women's sexuality; that is, black women have sex, as opposed to making love. It is important to reiterate that it *is* only a myth. Black women's sexual proclivities are no more or no less than those of white women, white men or black men. But it suits the purposes of perpetuating the myth to continue to behave as if they are different.

Realities

Incidence of incest and child sexual abuse

> Quite often, in a classroom, many women see how similar their oppressions have been. You will see how incest has permeated the lives of women – black women, white women, whatever – and the silence about that.[9]

In 1985 American psychologist Gail Wyatt, of the Neuropsychiatric Institute of the University of California, Los Angeles (UCLA), reported on the findings of her study on the sexual abuse of Afro-American [*sic*] and White American women in childhood.[10] It 'examined the prevalence of child sexual abuse in a multi-stage probability sample of Afro-American and White-American women' between the ages of 18 and 36, in Los Angeles County.

'The sample ranged in demographic characteristics by age, marital status, education and the presence of children. Of the total sample of 258 women 154 (60%) reported at least one incident of sexual abuse prior to age 18, with 54% of Afro-American women and 67% of White-American women having been abused.' The Wyatt study concluded that on the basis of the data: '1 in 2.5 Afro-American women experienced some form of abuse involving body contact as did 1 in 2 White American women.

'Based upon the result of this study, the profile of Afro-American women who are most at risk for child sexual abuse has been expanded upon from that developed in previous research,' notes Wyatt.

> Young Afro-American pre-teens are most likely to experience contact abuse in their homes, by mostly black male perpetrators, who may be nuclear or extended family members. Incidents involving non-contact abuse may occur in neighborhoods and be perpetrated by white men . . . In light of these findings for women 18 to 36 years of age, sexual abuse in childhood appears to be of equal concern today for Afro-American and white women alike.

Also in 1986, Professor Diana Russell, of Mills College in Oakland, California reported on her survey of 930 randomly selected women in San Francisco.[11] Of these 627 were white women; 90 Afro-American [*sic*] women; 66 Latina; 111 Asian and Filipina and 36 in other ethnic groupings. The corresponding rates of victimisation for participants were: white women (17 per cent); Afro-American women (16 per cent); Latina women (20 per cent); Asian and Filipina women (8 per cent); and other groupings (19 per cent). Russell noted however, that the differences between groups were small and not statistically significant.

In Britain the picture of sexual abuse of black women is even more patchy. A sampling of cases of sexual abuse reported to Southall Black Women's Centre between August 1989 and August 1990 revealed twenty-two enquiries involving sexual harassment. Amongst these were nine cases of incest or rape.

More recently, a study carried out in 1991 by the Child Abuse Studies Unit (CASU) of the Polytechnic of North London found that:

> one in two girls and one in four boys will experience some form of sexual abuse before their 18th birthday. In [our]

> survey of 1244 young people aged between 16 and 21, 59% of young women and 27% of young men reported at least one sexually intrusive experience before they were 18. Sexual abuse, here, is defined broadly including 'flashing,' being touched, being pressured to have sex and attempted and actual assaults/rapes. Abuse was committed by both adults and peers. Almost a third of these incidents occurred before the age of 12.[12]

The CASU survey also found that 'the prevalence rates for black and white women and men are the same'.

It is very difficult to obtain truly representative information on the incidence of sexual abuse in black communities. My purpose here is not to present hard and fast data. It is not about numbers, *per se*. Nor is the aim to produce a definitive or clinical study of the subject. It is to give an indication of what incest and other forms of child sexual abuse do to us as people and as black women. In the course of researching the book, I interviewed about a dozen black women – mainly African Caribbean – whose collective experience needs to be listened to and considered. Their stories also tell of our trauma, as well as our hopes; our sadness, as well as our fears.

I have tried to include as much secondary information as I could find – ideas of those who work with black women survivors, as well as any research that has been done with respect to black women survivors. My hope is that this material will contribute to a dialogue about incest and CSA amongst black people.

What is a survivor?

There are many different ways in which we survive. My intent here is to look at survival in terms of how I and other black women I've talked to have managed to deal with our abuse. I will not be using the names of the women whom I have interviewed for this book. Though they were all very willing to discuss their incest and sexual abuse, most, understandably, did not want to expose themselves to the extent that their names accompanied their stories. So in all cases, except where previously published information is used, survivors are not named.

Our stories are a cornucopia of coping strategies. Many of us have gone on to become successful at what we do; others have not. We all, however, have baggage. Some of us become over-achievers in an effort to overcome the feelings of degradation often associated with the incest:

> I decided that part of my life was over, so I wanted to achieve. I studied. I took an excellent degree. I thought, 'Right, if I can't be good in one way, then I'll be good at something else.' But deep down it doesn't get better and the more you suppress it, the worse it gets.

In my own case, I, too, became an achiever. In elementary school I got very good grades, I participated in school events – winning spelling bees and so on – and was considered a top student. In junior high school I became a member of the honour society and excelled in many subjects. In high school I got good grades, was an active participant in school activities and clubs, and read voraciously. In my senior year at high school I was voted Miss Congeniality, a title which conferred on me the mantle of a likeable and all-round student. All the while, at the back of my mind, I could not help thinking: 'What would all of these decent people think of me if they knew my secret?'

Others may go in the opposite direction:

> Right now, I'm not working. I haven't worked for five years . . . I've got no self-confidence. . . . My family tell me all the time I'm useless, good for nothing and a waste of time. My mum said to me: 'You went to college and you're wasting it.'

> . . . I know it's because of the incest. I always felt I'd never do well in life.

Sometimes the lines are not so easily drawn:

> I don't know if the desire for success started first or the effects of the abuse. In my village in Jamaica, my family told me I was the most beautiful girl in the world; that I was going to be successful; that I would put the village on the map.
>
> I don't know if I wouldn't have been the way I am anyway. There's part of me that feels it [the abuse] hampered me; because I was brought up with affirmation that I would make something of my life. It still feels like I may have done a lot of things a lot sooner if I didn't have all this emotional baggage.

All of us are traumatised in one way or another – whether it's emotional baggage; forming inadequate and unfulfilling relationships; dependency on drugs or an inability to wholeheartedly trust people or their motives. We cope by minimising the effects of our incest; denying it; rationalising it; forgetting it (or trying to); splitting our personalities; leaving our bodies (while it occurs); losing control; having chaotic lifestyles; being spaced out; being super alert; escaping; developing mental illness; self-mutilation; attempting (or being successful at) suicide; developing addictions or eating difficulties; lying, stealing or gambling; a compulsive need for safety at any price; avoiding intimacy; or compulsively seeking or avoiding sex.

It is, in short, a big deal for us, one that is not easily shrugged off, try as we might; and though we may indeed get on with our lives, it is often at a high cost to our fragile psyches, which can't forget or always suppress the pain.

The Russell study, which compared the long-term effects of childhood incestuous abuse on Afro-American [*sic*] and White American women in San Francisco found that:

> Afro-American incest victims . . . reported greater trauma as a result of the abuse than white incest victims. Possible reasons for this finding were discussed, including the fact that the abuse to which Afro-American victims were subjected was more severe in terms of the sexual acts involved, was accompanied by more force, and their incest perpetrators were more likely to be of an age associated with higher levels of trauma. In addition . . . the trauma of being raised an Afro-American female in a racist and sexist society may compound the effects of the abuse.

'Any woman who is not in a cemetery is a survivor,' note Carol Poston and Karen Lison in their book, *Reclaiming Our Lives.*[13] That is a good definition; it certainly holds true as well for black women. But it doesn't say it all. We need more than this. We deserve more. It is not enough simply to say that we're alive, so that means we coped with our abuse. What is important for us, as black women in particular, I think, is to feel that we can raise it as an issue, and that we can also count on the support of family or community members to help tackle all those skeletons in the cupboard. At the very least, we should not be ignored or silenced if we do raise it. Herein lie the recovery and wholeness which continue to elude many of us, whatever our state of survival.

Incest and racism

Incest exists. So, too, does the taboo against it. Black communities share this fact in common with other cultures and communities.

In *Betrayal of Innocence: Incest and its Devastation,* Susan Forward's and Craig Buck's discussion of the incest taboo notes that:

> Incestuous desires are in us all, though we engage in a variety of unconscious mechanisms to deny them . . . In

> our [Western] culture the incest taboo is taken as 'a matter of course.' If asked, the average person would say it would not be proper for a man to marry his mother or sister. But if asked why, he or she probably could come up with no better answer than 'Because it's wrong.'
>
> . . . almost all societies practice some type of incest prohibition. It must serve some purpose central to human society since almost every culture in history independently developed a form of the taboo.[14]

The brother–sister marriages of the pharaohs have been used to illustrate the supposed absence of fundamental genetic contraindications to incest, notes Jean Goodwin in her essay, 'Obstacles to Policymaking about Incest – Some Cautionary Tales'. 'However, recent re-examination of these lineages indicates that only two of the Ptolemies, one Hawaiian ruler and one Inca, were actual progeny of a brother–sister union.' It is likely that, as in African kingdoms that survived into the nineteenth century, the brother–sister marriage was a formal entity only; the king's unrelated wives, not the sister–wife, were designated for sexuality and procreation.[15]

It is important to discuss the taboo in black communities in terms of the effects of racism, because racism contributes to the maintenance of the taboo in these communities. Ideas that suggest incest and CSA are accepted practice do nothing to dispel views that it is normal for some black people. Nor do they challenge stereotypes about black people's sexuality. In addition, the taboo against speaking out about incest and CSA in black communities – crossing the boundary – may also be an outgrowth of an unwillingness to divulge that which is considered sacrosanct by our communities. Both aspects inform and help to explain the inaction that is apparent in our communities on the subject of child sexual abuse.

It seems that the taboo against fucking or fucking over little girls is outweighed (in some people's minds, at least) by a careful consideration of the constraints that racism imposes on black men. This reasoning suggests that black men have been denied much, because of racism. There is no doubting this. My point, however, is that an even bigger injustice and inequity arises when this is used as an attempt to apologise away or to rationalise the equally grievous outrage of incest. According to this reasoning, if respect for black men doesn't come from outside, then it had damn well better come from inside their homes and communities.

There are those who would include within this idea of 'respect' making sexual demands on their daughters, nieces, granddaughters. The fact that this is an obvious abuse of a power relationship is frequently lost. Consequently, on the occasions when black women survivors of incest and child sexual abuse do decide to speak out, it is at the risk of being charged with making our own families and communities even more vulnerable.

One woman I spoke to described her feelings:

> In our culture [African-Caribbean], we suffer not just the degradation, but the humiliation that it's happening to us in our societies. Because it fits the myths, the stereotypes they [white society] have of us. For a lot of women who don't and aren't able to acknowledge the abuse, it's linked with a feeling of not wanting to betray the community.

Beryl Gilroy feels the issue of the taboo in black communities is inextricably bound up with black people's history of colonisation and, in particular, black men's reaction to it. Historically, since slavery and other forms of colonisation, black men have felt a need to exhibit the male strength and power which is denied them in the wider community, and to compensate by demanding it within their own communities, by whatever avenues seem appropriate to them. 'Men work out their fury on the helpless,' said Gilroy. 'Who is the most helpless?' she asks. 'The child, and the sensations take over.'[16]

Speaking within the context of black women being expected to endure domestic violence in order to alleviate the stress of black men caused by oppression, black feminist Beth Richie-Bush has noted that:

> Undoubtedly, the stress black men endure is cruel and often overwhelming. The connection this has to black women accepting beatings puzzles me. Who is responsible? And where is the strength in acceptance? It is true that black women have historically been able to secure employment at times when black men could not. Does this make us any less oppressed? Why are we arguing whose oppression is worse?[17]

Another consideration, as Gilroy notes, is that it may be more appropriate to discuss incest in black communities in terms of child misuse rather than abuse, because the traditional scarcity of black women as a result of the ravages of slavery has fostered an attitude that, to some extent, acquiesced in regard to sex with children. As a result, some black men consider their children to be their possessions, and consequently have no remorse about their actions.

Added to this, though not simply in the context of black communities, is the fact that the idea of protecting children's rights still has some way to go when this is balanced against parental authority. Goodwin notes:

> [It] has been discussed at length how a child's legal rights to court protection and removal from parents can lead to years of shifting foster homes and permanent loss of developmental potential . . . Our system seems able at times to protect children against being sold into prostitution by parents, but we have much greater difficulty supplying . . . the advocacy and validation that could guide victimized children into

> their own chosen futures. Current controversies that develop out of this polarity include issues of enforcing parental custody or visitation on children who are violently opposed to the interaction.[18]

In Britain, the Children Act (1992) is an attempt to protect the rights of children, as well as to safeguard parental rights and authority. The jury is still out as to how well it does in getting the balancing act right.

Cause and effect

What are the consequences for continuing to ignore and/or excuse black men's abusive behaviour against women and children on the basis of their powerlessness in the face of racism? One survivor expressed her feelings this way:

> After my dad died, the thing that came out strongly was this: I can understand that we were poor; that he must have faced a lot of racism; that he was almost illiterate. He had all the dreams about coming here [from Jamaica]. I can appreciate all those things, and I can feel for him, but it's no excuse for abuse.

We actually help to *weaken* our communities by failing to challenge the predominantly accepted views that male authority must be achieved at the expense of female equality. In the end, we damage not only ourselves but future generations who perpetuate the myths and carry out these erroneous mandates. We make it that much harder for black women and children who are abused to seek and get the help they need, and to which they are entitled. One black woman said:

> There will always be those of us who uphold the taboo; and others of us who will raise it. My mother's anger [upon hearing of the abuse] didn't hurt me. When I told her, her reaction didn't surprise me. That's why the world's

> anger doesn't hurt me. It will take us [survivors] to say those things.
>
> We might not agree with it [breaking the taboo] but it's already out in the open. We need to be conscious that we're not the only ones who have dirty linen. I don't fear the stigma of disclosure – what I fear is that it will go underground in such a way that we can't detect it. For example, I know of one four-year-old who was told: 'I put a bomb inside you with my penis, and if you tell, it will explode inside you and kill you.' This kind of thing makes it no longer our little secret.

Beth Richie-Bush is a black feminist who worked for two years in a community-based agency carrying out grassroots organising for battered women in New York City. The agency's clients were 'predominantly black and Hispanic'. Many of the issues she has raised with respect to battered women are, I feel, also applicable to black women survivors of incest and sexual abuse, the common point being that both are excused by some in our communities on the basis that they are justifiable outlet valves for the stresses caused by racism. Stresses which are endured by black men, yes, but which occur in double doses for black women. Beth Richie-Bush writes:

> After a period of time, I gradually realised some of these strong, culturally-identified families, which we had been supporting so vehemently, were dangerous places for some women to live . . . I found myself caught in a trap, one which I have since learned may have been intentionally set for me. I can now recognise that this 'trap' is analogous to the 'trap' which many battered women find themselves in. It is the trap of silence.
>
> . . .The world is so hostile to Third World people that it seems much less painful to remain quietly ambivalent. I struggled with how to illuminate this dark secret about our homes and ourselves. Disclosure is so easily confused with treason!
>
> . . . Black women, be forewarned. It is a painful unsettling

> task to call attention to violence in our community. You may find yourselves feeling caught by the trap called loyalty. There is already so much negative information about our families that a need to protect ourselves keeps us quiet. Yet we must not allow our voices to be silenced. Instead we must strengthen and speak the truths about our families; we must support each other; but we must hear the cries of our battered sisters and let them be heard by others.[19]

Keeping quiet about abuse serves to reinforce it as a reality for black people, with devastating consequences. Witness, for example, the incident in July 1990 when 300 boys in a Kenyan school ran amok, raping and brutalising 71 schoolgirls and killing 19 others. One teacher was quoted as saying of the incident:

> Boys will be boys. It was, explained the teacher, just a prank that had gone wrong. The pupils had not wanted to cause trouble when they burst into the girls' dormitory. 'The boys never meant any harm against the girls,' she said. 'They only wanted to rape.' (*Observer* Magazine, 24 November 1991)

Breaking the silence – my story

My own incest happened, as near as I can remember, when I was 11 or 12 years old. My father was the perpetrator, as they say. It was not brutal or threatening. It simply was. I didn't know at the time (or, in fact, until much later) that it was called incest; or that it was abuse; or that it was punishable by law; or that it was something you survived. For me, it was just a part of what I experienced at a particular time in my life.

I did have a vague idea of feeling uncomfortable about my special closeness with my father; and I can remember thinking that probably no other little girls in the world were doing the same things with their fathers as I did with mine.

Not that they were very awful things in terms of being brutalising – I can remember being fondled by him, and of sitting on his lap and feeling his penis beneath me. These episodes took place most often when no one else was around. I don't remember them as being very frequent, as I come from a large family and there was nearly always someone else around.

I can remember feeling a closeness and warmth that was not always easily found in my family – though we were closeknit and there was love within it. Outward shows of affection, however, were rare and I can remember few hugs or kisses as a natural part of family life. When I became much older I found that establishing a closeness – a physical, touching closeness – with people was behaviour that I had to learn.

No, the way that affection was shown was through providing for us – by making sure we had food, clothes and 'a roof over our heads', as my grandmother used to say. That and a kind of self-deprecating humour amongst us were the outward signs of love, which we experienced as children, and which my brothers and sisters and I learned to accept as such.

That is why, I suppose, thinking back on it now, I accepted my father's clumsy and misguided attempts at affection. I don't remember him ever using force with me. His style was more one of gentle persuasion. He never penetrated me; but simply kept the act of the incest at what can best be described as the 'heavy petting' stage.

He was a charmer, my father. A good-looking man who was popular with women. He usually had a number of admirers on the go at any one time. During the time of our incestuous relationship, my parents' marriage was in the process of disintegration and there were ugly scenes when he was thrown out of the house, all his clothes landing in the street. Once, after one of these screaming bouts, my grandmother threw salt on my dad and he fled the house. It was a Sunday afternoon and he was taking us kids to the pictures at the local 'colored only' moviehouse. I can still remember the embarrassment of going down the street with him and brushing the salt out of his hair and off his clothes. In a way, and looking back at it now, I think I must have felt protective towards him, and thus receptive to his sexual advances. Maybe I even thought I was compensating for my mother's lack of interest in him – it could be so.

He used to say that the relationship was our secret. And that it wouldn't be good if anyone else in the family knew, because they wouldn't understand. I don't know if my father ever gave any thought to the moral rightness or wrongness of what he was doing. He may have done – on the other hand, his admonition to keep the secret may just have been an impulse to self-preservation.

Though, as I have said, there were not great displays of affection in our family, my father was the exception. He would demand and get kisses and hugs from us children, which we delighted in. He had a winning way and a disarming charm which made it hard to resist him.

The incest lasted a matter of months, rather than years. It seems, as I try and recall the pieces to fit them into place, that it happened during a time of great upheaval in my maternal grandmother's household, where we were all living at the time – mother, father and five children, along with my grandmother. In retrospect, I think I was, to some extent, trying to make up to my father for the failure of his and my mother's relationship.

After a time my father moved away, to another state. He went to California to seek his fortune, promising that he would send for us children when he had established himself. The incest stopped.

I never told anyone. Not until I was in my early twenties and confided to a very dear and much older woman friend who had become my mentor. Up until that time I had technically remained a virgin, as I had not been penetrated. I had also shied away from contact with boys, except for my two younger brothers, preferring to establish relationships with girls my age, but more importantly, with women – teachers, family friends, relatives, who nurtured and guided me. Interestingly, I also gained a reputation as a tomboy; I spent hours on my knees shooting marbles with my brothers and their friends.

I can also remember always being referred to as the 'good' girl in the family *because* I wasn't interested in boys. I worked hard at school, didn't date, and generally kept myself to myself as far as the opposite sex was concerned. I was known as the one who always had my head in a book. I read voraciously and built up a kind of idealised romantic world view in which the nastiness of sex, as I by now viewed it, did not intrude, except in a very sanitised way.

Thinking back on it now, I must have tried to compensate for the inward guilt and dirtiness I felt for having participated in such close sexual contact with my father. I always used to think it was ironic, and consequently felt consumed with guilt, that everyone thought I was the good one. My sisters were viewed as 'fast' for the harmless relationships they had with boys; while I, the supposed good one, had been far worse as regards my sexuality. For a long time I lived with a dread and a sick fear that somehow my secret would come out.

I was what you would call a late bloomer. Though there were boys who were interested in me, I managed to keep them at arm's length, through a combination of coolness and jokiness. I simply was not interested. Added to this was the fact that I also wasn't completely sure that I was still a virgin (there being no such thing as sex education at the time); and I did not know how I would explain it to my grandmother or anybody else if somehow it all came out that I wasn't.

When I was 20 I was raped by a right-on, progressive black

man, who was considered a pillar of the local community in Houston, Texas, where I now lived. I had become involved with the black/civil rights movement and had begun working for a grassroots community organisation of which he was the head.

He, again, was a good-looking, charismatic charmer – a ladies' man. At the time, he was involved with the woman whom I have earlier mentioned as my mentor. He used to engage in a kind of joky banter with me, which always contained sexual undertones. I regarded him idealistically as a brother committed to the black struggle. Though it would not be true to say I didn't find him attractive, neither would it be true to say that I, even for one moment, entertained the idea of a sexual relationship with him. Apart from the fact that he was sleeping with my friend, I was, by this time, afraid of having a sexual relationship with a man; and despite my 'experience' I was terrified and extremely naive about sex.

For his part, I think he regarded my friend's and my relationship as a threat to him somehow – to his virility, which was unquestioned in most quarters. Looking back on it now, I think it wasn't so much that he wanted me particularly – though the idea of another conquest (especially a suspected virginal one) probably entered into it – but that he had to prove to himself and to us that he was the dominant one; that the male/female relationship was far more important than our close female one.

It was a matter of pride to him, you see, that he came between me and what was unquestionably my best friend at the time. She was a woman who loved him and would have done anything for him, except forgive him for abusing me and betraying her.

He made his move one night when he took me home, after we had worked late in the office. The usual banter suddenly became something more sinister. He tried to force himself on me physically, and I fought. Finally, he played his trump card – he would go to this woman and tell her he didn't love her, had never cared for her, if I didn't acquiesce to his demand.

She was a woman whom I loved and valued, and I was terrified of what that would do to her; all I could think was that I didn't want to be responsible for her pain. It was a helluva dilemma, and in the end, he raped me.

I was far more traumatised by this than by the episodes with my father, which paled into insignificance by comparison. Afterwards, I was physically and emotionally ill. I went to see a doctor and told him that I had been raped. He examined me, confirmed that I had indeed had forceful sex, that the hymen was newly broken, and that I was traumatised.

I told him I was unsure about what to do next. My attacker was a well-known and respected member of the community and I wasn't sure I would be believed. Besides, all of this was taking place within the black community, and I had doubts about involving the police. The doctor said: 'Well, you know, it's always difficult to make these things stick.' He prescribed tranquillisers.

Because I had no one else to turn to, I told my friend what had happened. She challenged this man. But our friendship, though not destroyed, was damaged, which caused me almost as much upset as the rape. I left town soon afterwards and moved to California, and as there was nowhere else for me to go with no money, and being in a physical and emotionally traumatised state, I went to live in my father's house.

But I was no longer the pliable 12-year-old he had left behind, and I made it clear to him that I had no intention of being his sexual playmate any more. This he accepted, though it was not until years later, during a rap session with my sisters, that I subsequently learned why he was no longer interested in me.

I once challenged my father about the fact of our incest. He unconvincingly denied the whole thing. 'You don't know what you're talking about,' he said. When I persisted, he told me that if I continued to say those things, he would physically harm me. Not long after, I left his house, never to live under the same roof as him again.

We continued to have a cool and distant relationship – my father and I. He was even proud of me and my achievements, and would tell people about his eldest daughter who'd gone to college and was doing well for herself. Though tinged with this was his resentment and, I think, hurt that I never allowed him to get really close to me again.

After I had children, though they knew him as their grandfather, at least my son did, I never allowed them to stay with him on his own. By this time I had mellowed a bit towards him. He had become the patriarch of the family, and was loved by all his grandchildren as a gentle and affectionate man. I was always uncomfortable, however, that my sisters so readily and so freely allowed him to babysit for their children, with hardly a thought to his chequered history.

For my part, I was never quite able to relax with him again. I always felt an uncomfortable undertone because of what had happened between us all those years ago. I always had the feeling that he discounted my public person of goodness, because only he knew how bad I really was.

This was not overt or discernible to others. But sometimes I would catch him looking at me in a particular way, or speaking to me in a suggestive tone of voice, and it would all come flooding back, though I had tried so hard to put it in the far reaches of my mind. At times, I almost allowed myself to forget. But I couldn't quite. The ache of knowing what had happened and having to live with it dulled a bit at times in the passing years, but never, ever goes away.

I never spoke to my dad about the incest again. He died several years ago, and during his illness I went back to California to see him. I felt I had to broach the subject one last time somehow, and so wrote a long letter to him telling him my feelings about the incest, in an effort to try and lay it to rest with him. He was so ill by this time that I don't know if he ever read it.

I've always linked the incest with the rape. I suppose because it seemed to me that the fact of the incest somehow branded me as loose or easy or impure. I suppose, too, that it may have been mixed up in my mind with deserving to be raped for having lived the lie of being a goody for so long when I so clearly wasn't.

Unusually for me, I visited a *n'anga* (witch doctor) several years ago on a trip to Zimbabwe. The first thing he asked was: 'Why are you angry with your father?' He said my father's spirit could not rest as long as there was all this anger within me. I was completely taken aback, and decided then and there that perhaps if I laid my own anger with myself to rest, then maybe my anger against him would also dissipate. Committing my story to print, for myself and others, is my attempt at doing this.

Incest, black people and matriarchy

I have always been lucky to have very positive female role models in my life. My grandmother was and remains (even years after her death) the bedrock from which is hewn my value and belief system. A system which, though it has been honed and built upon during the course of my life, has remained pretty much intact as far as ideas of strength, integrity and caring about people are concerned.

She was a no-nonsense woman, not especially given to sentiment, who got on with the task of raising me and my seven brothers and sisters. She did it, in the main, single-handedly; just as she did most things, like building the small frame house which we lovingly and often with inverse, though loving, deprecation, called home in that deprived corner of an East Texas town.

For me, she was the premier woman amongst a host of strong women who peopled my childhood. They were the women who ran our community, which consisted of a few streets in a forgotten part of town that still did not have pavements in front of the houses when I left at the age of 20.

In addition to my grandmother, there was Cousin Sedonia, who lived at the top of our road in a quiet, cool house, where voices were seldom raised, who took care of her invalid husband, and worked as a trusted domestic for a local white family. It was Cousin 'Donia (as she was known by us) who helped to feed us when my grandmother's meagre earnings as the local seamstress didn't quite make ends meet. There was Aunt Pauline, who had a job at the local shipyard; there was quietly spoken Miss Kiddoe, who had a small house off the main road, and who told me it was all right for a little black girl from East Texas to like classical music; there was Miss Maggie, who lived next door, and kept cats, and who did not hesitate to give us kids a good talking to if she felt it was needed; there was Miss Lucy, for whom my grandmother made fancy dresses and who wore bright red nail polish. There was Miss Emma, Cousin Sarah, Mrs House, Miss Melba Boswell (my namesake) and many, many others, including, as I progressed through my all-black schools, black (mainly women) teachers who were genuinely concerned that their young charges should become the best and the brightest.

These strong, beautiful black women were my legacy. Though we were all undoubtedly poor (some more than others) it was not something we thought of as a dreadful state of affairs, at least not all the time. We were happy. We had food on the table most times; and we had a community to which we belonged. Looking back, I now know this was due, in large measure, to the fact that we knew we had these women to call upon, who could and did handle most situations, whether taking up a contribution to help pay someone's electricity bill, caring for the sick or taking in somebody's else's children to keep them from going to the county home.

The men who were around, including my father (whose time with us was spent in infrequent patches), were on the periphery. It was to my grandmother or one of the other women that we went if we needed anything or wanted to find out what was what. (I could not, however, go to my grandmother about the incest. Instinctively, I knew that to do so would court disaster, with her probably ending up killing my father and leaving us with no one.)

That was the way things were, and though sometimes I used to wish that we were a mythical nuclear family, with mother, father and brood of children (sort of a black 'Life with Father'), I never really entertained the idea for long. No, like it or not, and I most certainly did like and accept it, these strong, black women were my reality as a child. At the time, of course, I was not aware of any such thing as 'the matriarchal black community' – run by women, who, it would later be said, either drove away or emasculated their men into submission.

I was to learn, for example, of influential and intellectual whites like the Harvard academic Daniel Patrick Moynihan (a one-time presidential adviser to Richard Nixon). Moynihan had much to say about black communities and matriarchy. In the Moynihan Report (1965) he said it was the matriarchal nature of black communities that weakened them. 'The problem with blacks was not so much white racism as it was an abnormal family structure.'[20] Black communities were denied appropriate male role models because of the dominance of black women over black men; black women who had more education and who were able to obtain employment when the black man could not. This in turn helped to foster in black children a distorted view/image of black men.

My purpose here is not to debate the rightness or wrongness of the strong presence of black women in my childhood. It is a non-argument for me. They were there and I will forever be grateful and feel privileged that I had them to call upon. Without them – their nurturing, their affection, and yes, their sternness, I, and I know many others like me, wouldn't be here. I do feel it is important, however, within the context of incest and child sexual abuse, to ensure that these women don't take the rap for wrongs done in the name of male sexual gratification.

With incest, one argument in black communities is that had not black women been so busy being so strong and so all-doing – out there working two jobs, visiting or taking care of the sick, in church, or wherever – they might have been better able to see the abuse that was happening to their daughters under their very noses. The extension of this argument is that had the black matriarch/mother been around for her daughters and, more importantly, for her man, then he would not have had to look to his daughter to satisfy his sexual appetite.

There is evidence to show that many black women incest survivors do blame their mothers for the fact that they were sexually abused. (This idea of family dysfunction or mother/blame is discussed more fully in Chapter 5.) In my own case, I am satisfied that my mother did not know. She, too, was frequently absent from our lives, as children; like many black women of her time she was working hard, sending what money she could; and trying to reconcile her high hopes and limited possibilities as a black woman in an ever hostile world.

Some black women regarded themselves, and were

regarded, as substitutes for their absent mothers. One survivor said:

> I was my mother's substitute. It was a relief for her to know that he passed her bedroom door. He used to have to pass her bedroom to get to ours. He had to fuck her and beat her, so he just did it to us too – my sisters and me.

There is no doubt that some black women were and are aware of the sexual abuse of children. However, it is confusing and incorrect to use the presence of black women who were strengths in our communities as a basis for justifying the presence of sexual abuse by males. It does not change the very real fact that men are ultimately responsible for where they place their penises. It was my father's responsibility to set the boundaries, for me as well as himself. He chose not to.

To blame black women for the occurrence of incest and CSA is to overlook overwhelming evidence on who commits sexual abuse (see Chapter 5). It is also to let men off the hook. Those of us who feel the time has come for an acknowledgement of incest and CSA in our families and communities know that there can be no such acknowledgement until the men who commit incest first look to their own inability or unwillingness to hold their boundaries.

The question to be asked and answered by this is: 'Why did I allow my desire for sex to take precedence over my responsibility as a parent to love and protect this child in an acceptable and appropriate manner?' That, ultimately, is the bottom line.

CHAPTER 2

Incest in the work of black women writers

I went to hear the writer Buchi Emecheta at the Institute of Contemporary Arts in London shortly after the publication of her latest book, *Gwendolen*, several years ago. It was one of those meet-the-author sessions, where she conversed, read from the work and discussed what she meant to convey in it.

The book had been praised as a successful handling of incest in a work of fiction. I was interested to hear Emecheta say that although she had written about incest, the book was not about incest. It was about how to survive. 'You have to fight harder as a black woman,' she said. 'There is a lot of cultural energy in our communities which is being wasted because women are being put down.'

'I know so many Gwendolens,' she said later. 'I meet them all the time.' She went on to say that one workshop she had conducted included nine black girls, seven of whom told her of their abuse.

What struck me most about the session was first, her emphasis on survival – the fact that so much of who we are, of what frames the lives of black women, is conditioned by our capacity to survive. From somewhere within each of us, we manage to call upon centuries-old strengths which have enabled us to triumph over centuries-old adversities.

The second point about Emecheta's talk was that here again was another instance of a black woman challenging our orthodoxy with a dangerous knowing – in this case, revealing the trauma of incest in a black woman's life. Another black woman writer, to be more precise, who refused to play the game of silent acquiescence; an acquiescence which is content to allow incest to continue to be misconstrued and misrepresented as just a problem for the white community.

It occurred to me again that Emecheta was by no means alone as a black woman novelist who had chosen incest as a subject. As I began to go over the books in my mind and on my shelf, I began to realise that it is *only* in the work of these women that incest, and other forms of sexual abuse and violence against black women, appears consistently as a subject that concerns us as black people, and that ought to be on our agendas as communities.

I have to thank those women. For it was through and as a result of their work that I began to regard my incest as something more than just my problem alone. Here was the proof of people saying: this thing happened to me or to a woman I know. They had all eloquently defied the edict that you don't 'put our business out in the street', and survived that!

It was almost, therefore, with something approaching relief (if that's the right word) that I first began to read these women and to subsequently learn that 'it' wasn't just an aberration but that many, many others, just like me, had had the same or similar, or even worse experiences. It wasn't until I began to read these women that I was able to put my incestuous abuse into some kind of perspective. Though I had discussed the abuse to a small extent in my family, I still mainly regarded it as something peculiar to my family.

In deference and homage to the courage of those black

women writers, in this chapter I want to discuss the treatment of incest in the work of Buchi Emecheta (*Gwendolen*); Alice Walker (*The Color Purple*); Maya Angelou (*I Know Why the Caged Bird Sings*); Joan Riley (*The Unbelonging*); and Opal Palmer Adisa (*Bake-Face and other Guava Stories*). But before I begin, I would like to publicly thank these women for having the courage to break the taboo of silence, an outgrowth of which was to reach out to women like me, who needed their stories in order to find the strength to tell our own.

Maya Angelou, *I Know Why the Caged Bird Sings*: out of silence comes healing[1]

> 'A number of people have asked me why I wrote about the rape in *I Know Why the Caged Bird Sings*. They wanted to know why I had to tell that rape happens in the black community.' (Maya Angelou)[2]

Reading the first instalment of Maya Angelou's autobiography, more than twenty years ago now, was my first encounter with incest in the black community in print. Angelou was also one of the first black women writers I ever read, maybe *the* first. She, like Alice Walker with *The Color Purple* many years later, touched something in me.

I feel that this owes much to the empathy I have with their descriptions of rural, small-town black life. It was my reality too, growing up as I did in a small south-east Texas town (Beaumont, part of the Golden Triangle of oil- and rice-rich towns, along the Texas/Louisiana border, within spitting distance of the Gulf of Mexico). My part of Beaumont, though it was a town, had a distinctly poor and rural flavour to it, though it was within the limits of the city. In our part of town the roads were paved, but only just.

It was hardtop, a mixture of tar and rocks put down on sufferance. Sidewalks didn't exist, and when it rained the side roads became flooded, muddy quagmires of red clay.

I can remember, as a child going round to the little country-type store owned by one of the black families in our community. It was located at the end of one of these little dirt roads, and always smelt of kerosene. We could buy penny candy there that lasted all day, or huge moon cookies for a nickel, which were so big that they would easily equal two or three of a similar variety sold today (if you could get them, that is, which, of course, you can't).

I used to go to that little shop in the hot, humid and dusty Texas summers – barefoot, and kicking up the dust, and thinking I was surely the luckiest girl in the world to be allowed to 'keep the change' from whatever it was my grandmother had sent me for. It rarely amounted to more than a few pennies. But the delight in deciding whether to spend it on sweets or cookies or better still, saving up for a bottle of Coca-Cola from the Nehi Soda refrigerated box where the soft drinks were kept, makes me smile thirty-odd years later.

It was with an immediate kinship, therefore, that I read about such things as the red Coca-Cola boxes in Marguerite's (the young Maya's) grandmother's country store. For me, it was a validation of my own experience. It was then that I began the process of thinking about who I was and where I'd come from and what had contributed to me being the person that I was, in a serious way. I began to think of myself in a whole new way – as someone, if you will, whose experience counted for something. Began to feel that those everyday, ordinary things – which help to make up mine and the collective fabric of all black women's lives – were important to remember, record and pass on to those who came after. But even more importantly, here too was my experience of incest.

I shared with Angelou the reality of growing up in a household run by a strong grandmother, with only occasional stints spent with my parents. Marguerite's time with her grandmother (Momma) and Uncle Willie in Stamps, Arkansas, was in many respects not that far removed from my own with my grandmother Lucille in Beaumont, Texas. In each of those black communities we inhabited, we were brought up to be good, honest, Christian children, who respected our elders. Every adult member of the black community in Stamps (and in Beaumont) had the unmitigated right to tell us children how to behave, and if word got back to my grandmother that we were insolent or disobeyed, there would be 'hell to pay'.

Certain punishment, with no hope of any kind of negotiation, was the norm for daring to talk back, or cut our eyes or otherwise disobey an adult. And in those days, punishment was severe indeed.

When I got to the part where Marguerite was raped by her mother's boyfriend, Mr Freeman, I was stopped in my tracks. I was so surprised by it that I read and reread the passage. At first, I found it hard to believe. Though the characters and the setting were different, it came to the same thing – a young black girl like me, who was seduced 'in the Negro section of St. Louis', by a grown man from that community. It could have been me and my father, in the Negro section of Beaumont; for it awakened within me the same sense of guilt, fear and confusion that I had experienced as a child with my father. In the following passage, Angelou recounts the first occurrence:

> One morning she [her mother] got out of bed for an early errand, and I fell asleep again. But I awoke to a pressure, a strange feeling on my left leg. It was too soft to be a hand, and it wasn't the touch of clothes. Whatever it was, I hadn't encountered the sensation in all the years of sleeping with Momma. It didn't move, and I was too startled to. I turned

> my head a little to the left to see if Mr Freeman was awake and gone, but his eyes were open and both hands were above the cover. I knew, as if I had always known, it was his 'thing' on my leg.
>
> 'Now, I didn't hurt you. Don't get scared.' He threw back the blankets and his 'thing' stood up like a brown ear of corn. He took my hand and said, 'Feel it.' It was mushy and squirmy like the inside of a freshly killed chicken. He dragged me on top of his chest with his left arm, and his right hand was moving so fast and his heart was beating so hard that I was afraid that he would die . . . Finally he was quiet, and then came the nice part. He held me so softly that I wished he wouldn't ever let me go. I felt at home. From the way he was holding me I knew he'd never let me go or let anything bad ever happen to me. This was probably my real father and we had found each other at last. But then he rolled over, leaving me in a wet place and stood up . . . He came back with a glass of water and told me in a sour voice, 'Get up. You peed in the bed.' He poured water on the wet spot, and it did look like my mattress on many mornings.
>
> . . . Having lived in southern strictness, I knew when to keep quiet around adults, but I did want to ask him why he said I peed when I was sure he didn't believe that.

Freeman then threatens Marguerite by telling her he will kill her beloved brother Bailey if she tells anyone what happened. She keeps the secret, and before long begins to yearn for the closeness and warmth which Mr Freeman represented, to the point that she initiates the closeness, when he apparently shows no interest.

> I began to feel lonely for Mr Freeman and the encasement of his big arms. Before, my world had been Bailey, food, momma, the Store, reading books and Uncle Willie. Now, for the first time, it included physical contact . . . I began to wait for Mr. Freeman to come in from the yards, but when he did, he never noticed me . . . One evening when I couldn't concentrate on anything, I went over to him and sat quickly on his lap. He had been waiting for Mother

> again . . . At first Mr. Freeman sat still, not holding me or anything, then I felt a soft lump under my thigh begin to move. It twitched against me and started to harden. Then he pulled me to his chest. He smelled of coal dust and grease and he was so close I buried my face in his shirt and listened to his heart, it was beating just for me . . . He said, 'Sit still, stop squirming.' But all the time, he pushed me around on his lap, then suddenly he stood up and I slipped down to the floor. He ran to the bathroom.

Mr Freeman loses interest in Marguerite for months, and when she has even forgotten the closeness and warmth which she believed she was getting from him, he approaches her again with his 'mushy-hard' thing. When she refuses to be a part of his sexual game, he rapes her.

I was in my early twenties when I read the above passages. It was nothing less than a bombshell for me. How could she know those things? How could she describe the sensations I felt and actions I took with my father. I could remember, for example, going in search of my father and sitting on his lap, and feeling wonderfully close to him, while he, too, 'pushed me around on his lap'. The watershed I experienced was twofold: first, I began to think that this secret, which I'd kept so close to my bosom for so many years, was maybe, just maybe, a lot bigger than just me and my father. Secondly, it was then that I began the process of facing up to *all* of my feelings – including my feelings about enjoying the closeness and intimacy with my father.

It was a turning point for me. I learned from that book that you can face your demons, or at least begin to, and live to tell about it. The burden that lifted with that realisation is almost impossible to describe because it freed me to look at what happened between my father and me and to try and view it as dispassionately as I could, in a fledgling attempt to work through the guilt, blame and confusion.

I sometimes wonder if Maya Angelou can fathom the

magnitude of the great service she performed by writing the book. The power of those words, of seeing my experience verbalised, will remain one of my most unforgettable moments. I met her a few years later at a party in Berkeley. I was too shy then to tell her just how much what she had written meant to me. I wish I had.

Respecting your elders

Maya Angelou's book raises one issue which I think has a bearing on how incest is regarded in black communities. And that is the role of elders in our communities. As she notes in the text, her strict Southern upbringing didn't allow for questioning adults. It is doubtful, even without Mr Freeman's threat to kill Bailey, that Marguerite ever would have disclosed the secret and directly disobeyed an adult directive. It only came out after the rape plunged her into such sickness that hiding it was impossible.

Marguerite explains the dilemma children experience in the adult world when they are confronted with the 'Don't do as I do, do as I say' syndrome in their relations with adults. Following Mr Freeman's initial contact with Marguerite, when he accuses her of peeing in the bed, Marguerite thinks to herself:

> It was the same old quandary. I had always lived it. There was an army of adults, whose motives and movements I just couldn't understand and who made no effort to understand mine. There was never any question of my disliking Mr. Freeman, I simply didn't understand him either.

My point here is not to advocate the disrespecting of adults in our communities, far from it. But simply to say that it is important also to teach our children to be *discerning* as well as respectful. It is inexcusable to do otherwise, given what we know about the nature of incest and child abuse

– that some adults will abuse their privilege and power, simply because they can, and especially if it suits their needs (sexual or otherwise). It is counterproductive, and positively dangerous, to tell a child to respect all adults regardless of their motives. Such a position leads to confusion and hypocrisy, and ultimately, to a disrespect for adult authority which will eventually undermine the main point of the exercise – the building up of a strong and cohesive community.

One woman described to me her feelings on the subject of respecting elders:

> It has a lot to do with our belief systems. I always heard as a child: 'What happens in the home stays in the home.' 'You respect your elders and you don't talk back.' It affects children who should be encouraged to get help. But black families don't work in that way. There was no way I could go to anybody for help. There are also other ideas we instil in our children. Like, with friends of the family – we are told to respect what they do, no matter what. They don't always do good things, they do bad ones as well. We should look at the way parents work with children and perhaps they should try to address this.

This theme of disobeying black elders at your peril surfaces again and again in the work of black women writers as a central reason why many of our daughters keep quiet about their incest or abuse. In a story entitled 'Shoes', writer Pat Parker (another Texas home girl) relates an incident of abuse by a white store owner, in her childhood. An incident made worse by an order from her parents to obey adults, without question, especially white adults. Of the story, Parker said:

> I felt the need to get it out of my system in order to move on to other things. I had never told the story to anyone. I carried a great deal of anger as a result of the incident: anger towards my parents for their insistence that I respect any

> adult as an authority figure; anger towards the store owner for his perversion and use of me; and anger at the economic structure of this political system.[3]

Though Parker writes about black life in 1960s Texas, a similar time frame to my own story, what we both experienced as black youngsters being schooled in the etiquette of home truths was that adults, even if they were wrong, were always right. Ought we not to be at least as concerned with protecting our children, and their rights, as we are with protecting the sometimes questionable integrity of grown-ups?

We could begin by instilling in our children a sense of their value as people, as equal partners in the sense that they have a responsibility to themselves as well as to their communities; and that paramount among their rights is not to be interfered with in an abusive way. As adults, we too have a responsibility to ensure that, at the same time as we are teaching them respect for their elders, they also learn the importance of their place within those communities, and that their right to an unfettered existence is as sacrosanct as the next person's.

It is not always easy to find the balance between rights and responsibilities. But within the context of child sexual abuse, especially, we fail to attempt it at our peril. The powerlessness and frustration that children feel, especially black children, who are often raised in a strict disciplinarian fashion requiring unquestioning obedience, is real. When the issue of sexual abuse is added to this dilemma it can lead to confusion and alienation.

If we do not begin to recognise this fact, we risk losing our children. We *are* losing them, as they find it difficult to reconcile the reality with the rhetoric. We may find that all attempts at preserving the integrity of our communities will be overshadowed. The very values we are trying to impart, often with the best of intentions, will become as extinct as the dinosaurs.

Alice Walker *The Color Purple*: substitution and repairing self-image[4]

Reading Alice Walker's *The Color Purple*, for the first time – getting to know fourteen-year-old Celie, who suffers her father's sexual intrusions – opened my eyes further to the likelihood that sexual abuse was not quite the rarity I had supposed it to be.

I read it, fascinated. I could not put the book down. Here, again, was the life of another ordinary black girl from the South, loved by her sister, abused by her father, and left to try and make sense of her situation. In much the same way as *Caged Bird* had ten years earlier, *The Color Purple* touched something in me. It was difficult to express all the emotions the book aroused – anger, frustration, despair, respect, hope, love, dignity, and just plain happiness, are just a few.

Here, again, was a black woman, a talented black sister writing our story; putting down memories and fragments of memories, culled from an almost forgotten black and female past. Of which memories American writer Mary Helen Washington once said: 'We didn't suspect [they] . . . were important enough to write books about, and yet these were our lives, the black woman's unspoken truths.'[5]

And here again was incest. In Alice Walker's story Celie does not know what is happening to her. She does not understand the changes which her body undergoes – assault and eventual pregnancy by her father. She knows only that her mother, worn out from having babies, wants to be left alone, and that she is then propelled into the role of the surrogate to receive her father's unwanted sexual advances.

Celie's father twice makes her pregnant. Though the two pregnancies are never discussed, her mother goes to her grave cursing her, and perhaps cursing herself for knowing this is happening to her daughter and for being unable to prevent it. Celie must endure her mother's curses, and her father's sexuality and condemnation. She also endures him separating her from her children to an unknown fate. Through it all, she puts her trust in God.

I was in the Brixton Black Women's Group when *The Color Purple* came out. At the time, we wrote collectively about its effect on us as black feminists:

> It is not like a story because you instinctively feel the truth of it . . . But like most stories you know it is derived from Every Black Woman. In trying to create a black feminist critical analysis [we look for] . . . how . . . sexism, racism and black female identification occur. Also for the use of a specific, black female language – lesbian/ woman-identified relationships (as central, pivotal and positive), self-definition and the discovery of the limitation of black women's prescribed role.
>
> Within 'The Color Purple', all these aspects are explored – black identity in the harsh, segregated world of the South, is a prerequisite for survival in the sense of having to know your place (or not), as in the case of Celie's friend Sofia and her Amazonian sisters. Their experience was [that] of being 'pore black women' and retribution for daring to bring any pride to these aspects of their lives. Sexual and racial politics account for the rape of Celie by the man she knew as her father, for her sister Nettie being forced to leave; for Celie's loss of her children and her marriage to a man she does not know, love or enjoy sexually. These combine to restrict her growth in all dimensions. 'Life' is narrowed to day-to-day existence and the acceptance of her 'fate'.
>
> Discovery of this narrowness and self-definition comes through the letters of Nettie from Africa, which show that she is not alone in her experiences. Also, through the love and friendship of the other Black Women in her community, she is allowed the freedom to express herself.[6]

Two things stand out for me with respect to the book – the whole idea of the self image which black girls grow up with; and, with regard to Celie's being raped by her father, the issue of substitution.

Some of the most enduring memories from my childhood concern how I looked and regarded myself as a black girl. I had nappy hair, which had to be straightened every week with a hot comb. It was plaited during the week to keep it under control. This was during a time when plaits were definitely not in fashion, as they are today as black women have, thankfully, increasingly come to redefine beauty within an African context. I can remember, as I'm sure many young black girls can, in those bygone years, the practice of putting a towel on my head and swinging it around, pretending I had long, straight hair, like the white girls I saw on TV.

It is sad, but true, that many of us – not all, but many of us – grew up thinking that our bodies were not beautiful because they didn't fit the white, and therefore accepted image of beauty. It was either that our skin was too black; our bottoms too big; our hands too rough; our lips too thick; our tongue too harsh; or our voices too loud. None of it, however, represented beauty as we knew it then. In a discussion of the impact of black women writers in helping to change these misconceptions, writer Mary Helen Washington said:

> As we investigate these stories, certain recurring patterns emerge that tell us a great deal about the uniqueness of the adolescence of the black girl. Almost without exception, these writers describe the black girl's growing up period as essentially unprotected. They show the black girl developing self-reliance and resilience in order to deal with the hostile forces around her, quite often assuming adulthood earlier than she should have to because of the external pressures around her.[7]

We grow up, many of us, thinking that we are worthless. Probably many of us who have been sexually abused feel this is no more than we can expect. We grow up thinking in our heart of hearts that maybe we don't deserve better because our faces don't fit and our attitude is not right. In short, that *we* aren't *right*.

That is why Celie does not question her father – not when he abuses her and makes her pregnant, not when he takes her children, not when he forces her into a marriage she does not want. She accepts it all as her due – marriage to Mister and more abuse and degradation. She accepts it because until then her self-image is governed by her father's perception of her as ugly and dumb.

Celie's father uses this negative self-imagery to justify the abuse – sexual and otherwise. It becomes necessary for him to try to reduce her to the status of a lowly object because not to do so would mean having to take responsibility for his actions.

The negative self-imagery continues with the marriage to Mister. He treats Celie as a domestic servant, there to periodically service his sexual needs and to keep his house clean. Eventually, however, Celie begins to learn the beauty of her black womanhood – through the friendship and love between herself and Shug Avery. They both grow as individuals, and through their love, come to the self-discovery and self-determination which is their true legacy, rather than the sacrifice and self-hate that has been mapped out for them.

If we are lucky, as black women – whether we are survivors of sexual abuse or not – we reach a point where we no longer feel the need for a towel on our heads; we no longer agree to lying down and taking whatever the male ego thinks we deserve; but instead glory in the rich heritage that is ours and in the knowledge that we are worthy of and capable of more than someone else's misguided perceptions of who we are.

Substitution

I don't know if I consciously considered myself a substitute for my mother when I did not object to the intimacy between myself and my father. Looking back on it now, I may have done. My situation was not like that of Celie, though my mother, too, had had a number of children by my father. I don't know if she regarded sex with my father as a burden or a chore. I only knew that they were getting on badly and he seemed to be in pain.

This idea that we as black women have, of feeling we must shoulder the burdens of the world, is also part of our heritage. 'From the intricate web of mythology which surrounds the black woman, a fundamental image emerges writes Michele Wallace in her book *Black Macho & the Myth of the Superwoman*.

> It is of a woman of inordinate strength, with an ability for tolerating an unusual amount of misery and heavy, distasteful work. This woman does not have the same fears, weaknesses, and insecurities as other women, but believes herself to be and is, in fact, stronger emotionally than most men. Less of a woman in that she is less 'feminine' and helpless, she is really more of a woman in that she is the embodiment of Mother Earth, the quintessential mother with infinite sexual, life-giving, and nurturing reserves. In other words, she is a superwoman.[8]

As a little girl, growing up in a predominantly female household, I know something of this burden that black women carry. It has become ingrained in my psyche. In her novel, *Their Eyes Were Watching God,* Zora Neale Hurston, an important black American novelist of the 1930s, includes a character who is – 'an old grandmother, a former slave bought and sold like a bag of rice and forced to raise a granddaughter in the white folks' backyard'. Of the black woman's position, the grandmother says: 'De nigger woman is de mule uh de world so fur as Ah can see.'[9] As a twelve-year-old, I did not fully understand the implications of what it meant to carry the black woman's burden. Certainly I understood it in terms of assuming some responsibility for helping my grandmother to run our household. But sexual responsibility? Maybe it was also my father's expectation that this was not out of place either. I don't know.

As a thirty-year-old reading *The Color Purple*, however, I began to make some connections. One recurring theme among many of the women with whom I've spoken in preparing this book has been their feelings that their abuse was somehow connected with being regarded and regarding themselves as substitutes for their mothers.

'It was a relief for her to know that he passed her bedroom door,' said one woman. Another added:

> When I was 13, my dad started apologising for the abuse. He said it was because I was the image of my mother when he first met her. A lot of it felt displaced. I feel I am the image of my mother. I can remember my father crying when he abused me and saying sorry . . . After the row [about disclosure] when I was 18, me dad said I had to go. He said: 'I can't have two women and I'm married to the one upstairs.' My mom cried when I left and everybody felt sorry for her. Everyone blamed me for my mother's crying; but she had told my dad if he did not throw me out she would leave. I couldn't tell anybody. No one would understand.

We may look like our mothers, act like our mothers, laugh like our mothers, even have the same shape as our mothers. Our mothers may be tired from working too many night shifts; disillusioned by too many lost opportunities; or worn out from childbirth. None of it gives the men in their lives – whether they are our fathers, or as artist Sonia Boyce called them, 'a Mr Friend of the Family'[10]

– the right to use the bodies of their daughters as a kind of vast pond of female flesh that is available to them, to use as they like.

Whether it was done lovingly or not does not enter into it. The thing to remember here is that these men abused not only our bodies, but also the position entrusted to them as adults responsible for the care and nurturing of us, their daughters. It has to do with what psychotherapist Sonia Francis calls 'the patheticness of men who cannot hold their boundaries'.[11] It has to do with an inability or an unwillingness to make a judgement that goes beyond immediate gratification. It is about, says Francis, 'addressing the men, because ultimately, they're responsible for where they put their dicks, regardless of whether the abuse was brutal or loving'.

Buchi Emecheta, *Gwendolen*: survival against the odds[12]

Gwendolen is an innocent – as we all were. She is also a survivor – as we all are. Though she is not meant to, she does survive.

The story begins with life in rural Jamaica. Gwendolen lives with her Granny Naomi, following her beloved parents' departure – first her father, followed a few years later by Mother – to England, in search of work and a better way of life.

When she is nine she is raped, for the first time, by Uncle Johnny – 'a Mister Friend of the Family'. It is the first of many such occasions with him. Uncle Johnny helps her Granny Naomi and is a great support to her amidst the grinding poverty that forms the backdrop to their lives. He tells Gwendolen it's their secret.

Though Gwendolen resolves to tell her grandmother of the incident, events intervene and the abuse continues. At last she runs away, and returns to finally disclose what has been happening.

She is believed. Her Granny and the community rally around Gwendolen, accuse Uncle Johnny and heap scorn and condemnation upon him. But when it emerges that the abuse has occurred over a period of time, doubts about her role and her sexuality creep in. The men suggest that, 'Maybe, the lill marm love the job . . . The women still defended her, though their voices of protestation were taking a lower key.'

Gwendolen eventually leaves Jamaica – abused, illiterate, and isolated when her parents send for her from England. She arrives to a cold climate and a warm reception from her father who comes to meet her. The eldest of her parents' (by now) four children, she is sent for (though she doesn't know it) primarily because of the need for a second pair of women's hands in the household.

She does not take to school and is a slow learner. But she is a good girl, and still an innocent, despite her prematurely enforced sexuality. The occasion of an extended trip by her mother back to Jamaica on the death of her Granny provides the opportunity for her father to abuse her.

He regards Gwendolen as just like her mother. But also, because of their long years spent apart, he views her only as his biological, and *not* his social daughter, unlike her sister. He pounces – expecting to meet resistance as, he notes: 'After all women were expected to do that – ward men off.' But Gwendolen, mindful of the outcome of her previous experience with Uncle Johnny, and fearful of the consequences if she tells again, submits, much to her father's surprise. He regards her submission as stupidity and views it as her failure to see through the sexual cajolery.

Gwendolen is shattered that her beloved father can do this to her in the same way that Uncle Johnny did. She does not understand why he commits the act, nor his anger and 'disappointment' when he learns she is not a virgin; nor his hypocrisy when he preaches in church the next day about the evils of sin. Inwardly, she does not recover from the confusion.

Eventually she is made pregnant by her father. Her mother returns and blames her. Unable to endure the tension and discontent which has replaced the joviality in the household, Gwendolen runs away and ends up admitted to a mental institution for her failure to talk or disclose any information about herself. When her mother and father finally come to visit her in the institution, she is mute – with anger about her abuse, with the guilt of it, and from the incomprehension which envelops her as she tries to understand adult motives and sensibilities. Still, she does not accuse her father, because of her fear of being ostracised and disbelieved. She resolves both to have the child she is carrying and never to live under the same roof as her father again.

Gwendolen's father, consumed by the guilt of what he has done, but unable to admit it to his wife or his daughter, is prophetically killed in an accident on his construction site. Gwendolen gives birth to a beautiful daughter, Iyamide, who is the image of her father.

Gwendolen survives because she must for her daughter. She survives with the help of her few friends – Emmanuel, the misfit Greek boy who teaches her to read and who is initially mistaken as her baby's father; her mother's friend Gladys, a Nigerian, who guesses the truth and recognises Gwendolen's pain and suffering; and a sympathetic nurse in the hospital. Gwendolen is able to begin the long road back to recovery. For the first time, since being raped by Uncle Johnny at the age of nine, she is able to think of herself as someone deserving of love, affection and respect.

Joan Riley, *The Unbelonging*: thwarted humanity and sexuality – the survivor as victim[13]

Hyacinth Williams, Joan Riley's heroine in *The Unbelonging*, is a victim. She survives the threatened sexual advances and the relentless physical abuse from a brutal father, the racism of a hostile England and the searing homesickness for her beloved Jamaica. But though she survives, she loses something of her humanity, her ability to connect with the world. Hers is a life lived in heart-wrenching isolation, containing only unfulfilled and unfillable dreams and nightmares.

Hyacinth is not a whole person. She is emotionally damaged, unable to form whole relationships or even to accept friendship when it is offered. She is victimised by the guilt and shame she feels at being black; at being abused; at being different.

I found it difficult to relate to Hyacinth, *because* she wore the badge of victim with such ferocious determination. Her refusal to recognise reality was alien to me. Her inability to let go of a past that was so apparently hopelessly out of the bounds of her reality or any reality (apparent that is, to everyone except Hyacinth) was almost too painful to bear. It was perhaps, her way of managing the brutality which she found upon her arrival in the strange country of whites. But the shroud of her pain left no room for anything else.

There is little doubt that her reality, once she is taken away from her beloved Jamaica and brought to England, is a harsh one, characterised by thinly disguised racism, contempt and outright brutality. The manner in which Hyacinth is able to deal with it, however, belies the notion of the strong black woman and conjures up instead, the role of the hapless victim. The school of hard knocks is something we all know about, as black people. But we do not have to become victimised by it to the extent that *we* lose sight of who we are. Unfortunately for Hyacinth, she does lose sight of who she is, with the result that she is unable to acquire the tools with which to extricate herself from the role of victim.

Hyacinth is unwillingly brought to England at the age of eleven, by her father, whom she does not know, to live with him, her stepmother and two stepbrothers. From the moment she arrives her life is hell – from the shock of seeing 'the sea of white faces everywhere, all hostile', to the dawning realisation that she will have to endure the brutality of life in England, not the least of which are the beatings inflicted by her father to discipline her.

Hyacinth copes by escaping into dreams at night – dreams of her beloved Jamaica and her Aunt Joyce. She retreats into an idealised re-enactment of life in the back streets of Kingston and the childhood games and fantasies of an eleven-year-old. Unfortunately for Hyacinth, reality intrudes, and the stress of life in England, with an unloving stepmother and a brutal father in an environment of poverty and racism, proves too much.

She copes with the pain of separation by constant bedwetting, which causes her father's brutal treatment to escalate into a sickening spiral of violence almost to the point of her death. Each time she awakes from her dreams she does so to her father, who takes a perverse pleasure in inflicting pain upon her frail body. The beatings become worse, until they reach a point (in one particularly brutal encounter) when Hyacinth is kicked down the stairs and fears she will die.

She does not die. She survives the beating, and many more, always, however, retreating further and further into herself and her memories of Jamaica for comfort. Hyacinth is without friends. There is no consolation at school, where she becomes the butt of racist ridicule and bullying from her classmates, and suffers studied indifference from teachers, who, though aware that things are not as they should be for her, choose not to get involved in the lives of an unwanted immigrant population.

Hyacinth's father's attitude changes towards her once she begins to menstruate. He becomes softer, more suggestive in his approaches to her. Eventually he makes his move. He tells Hyacinth that he wants to be the one to school her in the ways of sex, so that she is not taken advantage of. 'I going to show you some of the things not to let men do,' he says to her.

Incest flourished where the roads were bad. This line appears in a book given to Hyacinth by her stepmother. The book had belonged to a girl cousin, who underlined the crucial passage. The girl had lived in Hyacinth's father's house. As she begins to discover its meaning, Hyacinth feels increasingly threatened by 'the lump' which appears in her father's trousers each time he beats her or suggestively tries to get close to her. Her feeling of desperation is heightened after her stepmother flees the house, following a merciless beating by Hyacinth's father because she had attempted to protect Hyacinth.

The sickening realisation of her father's intentions towards her are confirmed when he tries to rape her. Hyacinth manages to fight off his drunken and frenzied attempts to sexually abuse her. She too flees, never to see her father again.

She is eventually taken into care. Her remaining years to adulthood are spent in an all-white children's home and later, when she is no longer a child, in a hostel for ex-offenders – all of it lived against an unrelenting racism and ever-deepening isolation. Hyacinth does not form relationships with black people because she cannot accept and bitterly laments her own blackness; a blackness which has marooned her in a hostile white world.

She cannot form relationships with whites because she is all too aware of the racism that is ever-present, and which ensures that her father's caution – 'The don't like neaga here' – is etched in her brain. Memories of her father intrude to make relationships with black men out of the question; she hates their blackness, their sexuality, their perceived menace.

Hyacinth becomes locked in her own isolation and feelings of guilt. She has no one in which to confide, and retreats deeper into her daydreams. She decides that education is her way out of England and proceeds to achieve academically, gaining a degree in chemistry at university in Birmingham.

Although she begins to allow one or two black people in at the margins of her life, her isolation and ignorance about the world soon become apparent. In particular, the reality of life in Jamaica proves a further wedge between her and one of the two black friends she is eventually able to make. Perlene, whom Hyacinth meets at university and who is also Jamaican, attempts to question Hyacinth's idealised vision of their country, and is met with rebuff and derision.

Charles, a Zimbabwean postgraduate student who loves Hyacinth and understands her homesickness and isolation, is also met with rejection when he makes love to her. His efforts are doomed because he has no knowledge of the years of abuse, numbing isolation and self-loathing which have made up Hyacinth's world.

At last Hyacinth returns to Jamaica, and is amazed to find that it has changed beyond recognition. She is stung by the fact that she does not belong there either. But locked as she is into herself, she has no one and nowhere to turn, no identity – she belongs nowhere.

Her life becomes a metaphor for oppression, humiliation and isolation. As the book ends, we are not sure whether Hyacinth will survive – spiritually, emotionally or in fact.

Writer Mary Helen Washington once said:

> We need stories, poems, novels and biographies about black women who have nervous breakdowns, not just the ones who endure courageously; stories about women who are overwhelmed by sex; wives who are not faithful; women experiencing the pain and humiliation of divorce; single women over 30 or 40, trying to make sense out of life and perhaps not being able to.[14]

In Hyacinth, we have such a heroine. It is not her fault. The experience of Hyacinth could be that of us all if we were to lose sight of the humanity that is the other side of our stories. As black people, *we* know (or ought to know) that the stereotype is not the reality. We know that racism and abuse are only aspects of our histories, our stories.

We may falter. Historically, however, we have never given up as a people – not on ourselves, nor our hope for the future. There is no reason to believe that we ought to give up on the idea of doing something about incest and CSA. Such a recognition does not penetrate Hyacinth's despair and hopelessness. Hyacinth's abuse robbed her of hope to the point that she is unable to reach out and touch the hand of humanity – black humanity – with an expectation that it will be grasped with the friendship and love she surely deserves.

I hope there are not too many Hyacinths out there – I know there are some: girls and women who may be lost to us because their despair, like Hyacinth's, is so great. It is too late for some. My hope is that the voices which are raised among us will help to break through the walls of silence to lessen the despair.

Opal Palmer Adisa, *Bake-Face and other Guava Stories*: choice and friendship

> The first time her uncle raped her, she was twelve and already seeing blood, so she feared all month but nothing happened and he kept on, and others took their cue from him and used her like the soil, but her stomach remained close to her back.[15]

Bake-Face, the heroine of Opal Palmer Adisa's story, is a silent woman. It is a silence which carries with it unrequited passion, and a resignation to her circumstances, yet tinged with a desire to take control of her life, in some way, before it is too late.

Her silence begins from the age of 10, when she is orphaned and sent to live with aunts and uncles who physically and emotionally abuse her. Like Joan Riley's Hyacinth, she retreats within herself, wearing her silence as a badge of defiance. Unlike Hyacinth, Bake-Face's silence is not the silence of deafening despair; she is a woman aware of what is missing in her life and is willing to take a chance on getting it – at least once.

Accused by her aunts of 'spreading her legs for her uncles', Bake-Face recognises that they 'could not protect her or disobey themselves'. She is rescued by Ezra, who tells her: 'Ah ave four bwoy dem; dem is good. Las yam season ah put me wife in de ground. Ah need someone fi help wid de house; yuh will get food, shelter an change, no abuse.'

Bake-Face leaves the house of her uncles and aunts and goes to live with Ezra, who is as good as his word. Eventually they marry and she settles down and resigns herself to a life of cooking, cleaning, and occasional sex with Ezra, whose needs are not great. In the course of time, Bake-Face has a daughter, Pauline, after having given up hope that she can bear children.

It is as a result of Pauline's illness that she meets Frank Johnson in a hospital, and begins to think for the first time that this is the chance she has been waiting for.

Bake-Face and Frank are attracted to each other, recognising a kindred spirit which requires acknowledgement and fulfilment. Bake-Face agrees to go, with Ezra's knowledge, to live with Frank (who is also married) for five months of the year as seasonal workers during the sugar-cane harvest on an estate, where they live together as man and wife. Here, each fulfils the other's need for the passion and love that is missing from their lives the other seven months of the year, and which has eluded them throughout their lives.

Bake-Face gives herself to Frank Johnson fully and without regret, satisfying the need they both have to grab a piece of life before it is too late. After five years of their relationship, however, she begins to yearn for more – to regard herself as worthy of more.

Bake-Face eventually chooses to return to Ezra and her family. It is a conscious, though difficult, choice for her. But it is one which she herself chooses to make; not one that is thrust upon her by circumstance. It is a decision which takes her further from the passive state of silent victim to the positive role of affirming herself – her future, her life, her choice. Though she remains silent, being a woman of few words, it is not the silence imposed by a life lived without hope or love. It is a silence which says: 'I have faced life squarely and made my choices. This is how I choose it to be. This is how it will be.'

Another aspect of Bake-Face's life with Frank Johnson on the plantation is the richness of women friends she comes to know and appreciate for the first time. The women who share the yard of the seasonal housing offer each other love, support and companionship in the face of adversity in the see-saw relationships with their men. The women argue amongst themselves, but for the most part it is done with an understanding of the underlying love and affection.

Bake-Face learns to share her life with the other women. She learns the joy of sisterhood – a sisterhood which is born out of acknowledged needs and desires. Their talk is of their relationships with the men in their lives; the work of bringing up their children. It is also about the joy of relating to each other as women, in the way that only women can:

> At the showers, Bake-Face is greeted by Jennifer who is singing another sassy calypso at the top of her voice. Bake-Face smiles at Jennifer, feeling somewhat akin to her. They hold each other around the waist and dance a few steps; Joyce watches them, then joins in the fun. Before long, the five women are singing at the top of their voices and doing a jig. Some man hollers: 'Damn blast ooman, dem nuh gi yuh rest a nite an marnin dem start dem noise, like is dem one know good time.' The women fan their hands in the direction of the voice and continue their song. Then they return to fixing breakfast. Bake-Face declares, 'Jennifa, gal, ah gwane mek yuh some ah de bestest blue-drawers fore ah leabe.' The women rejoice, singing as they work. Bake-Face is long in the shower. Everything is right; she can leave now.

It is her ability to recognise and accept these relationships with the women of Bruk-Up yard which enables Bake-Face to transcend the silence imposed by years of abuse – emotional and sexual – and to find the strength that is always within her to name her own destiny.

CHAPTER 3

Black women, sex and sexuality

> I used to speak in the smallest voice, so as not to draw attention to myself – to my body, my sexuality. (Black woman at a conference workshop on black women and sexual abuse)

The aura surrounding black women's sexuality has much to do with the scenario surrounding incest and how it is perpetrated. As black women, we grow up with an awareness of preconceived assumptions about our natures as sexual beings. Such assumptions about women's sexuality are not peculiar to black women. Male assumptions about sexuality affect all women, regardless of race.

Without doubt these myths, for that is what they are, govern how men view women generally. Feminist writer Adrienne Rich has said that:

> Fundamental to women's oppression is the assumption that we as a group belong to the 'private' sphere of the home, the hearth, the family, the sexual, the emotional, out of which men emerge as adults to act in the 'public' arena of power, the 'real' world, and to which they return for mothering, for access to female forms of intimacy, affection, and solace unavailable in the realm of male struggle and competition.[1]

However, the myths surrounding black women's sexuality are qualitatively different from those assigned to white women. White women, for example, are sexy; black women are animals. White women are pretty; black women are exotic. White women are promiscuous; black women are sluts.

Sexual stereotyping

The stereotypes which flow from these assumptions are endless; and almost all have negative or passive connotations. For example, we

- are always ready
- provide the best sex
- are exotic creatures of passion
- have bodies that are just too sexy for words
- can't get enough of it
- are over-sexed
- are used to it.

Any consideration of black women's sexuality must also be bound up with the 'peculiar double consciousness' whose basis lies in racism, and to which all black people in a predominantly white society must adjust. Incest and sexual abuse must be looked at against this backdrop – for, as black women, we are framed within the collective consciousness on the basis of our blackness and our gender. It has to do with racism; it has to do with control and the lack of control; it has to do with a lack of respect for us as black women. To white men, we are exotic and passionate, knowing what there is to know about how to please a man. Some black men share these perceptions of us. But the added dimension when it comes to black men is that we are also their mothers, their sisters and their daughters.

That ought to bring with it different attitudes about black women based on a mutual history of exploitation and racism – attitudes which, you would have thought, would go beyond a superficial acceptance of stereotypes. Too often, however, it brings the opposite and results in the perpetration of acts which further exploit black women, sexually and otherwise. It also results in a failure to acknowledge the abuse that is taking place, and involves an even greater propensity to keep it hidden. What this engenders is an attitude both within and outside our communities which reinforces the stereotypes.

It becomes, in effect, a self-perpetuating spiral. It is unfortunate that some black men take their cue from white society's definitions about who we are as black women. In other words, they buy into the accepted (male) view that places black women as fair game in their pursuit of sexual pleasures. They parcel us off into body parts, forgetting the thinking, feeling, and caring aspects of who we are, and forgetting also that our destinies are inexorably intertwined. If we are objectified, they too will be victimised by stereotypes in the wider society. If black women's survival is threatened, so too is that of black men.

Billie Holiday, in her autobiography, *Lady Sings the Blues*, talks about the damage that stereotypical victimisation can cause when she describes the aftermath of her rape by one of her neighbours:

> But that wasn't the worst of it. The cops dragged Dick off to the police precinct. I was crying and bleeding in my mother's arms, but they made us come along too.
>
> When we got there, instead of treating me and Mom like somebody who called the cops for help, they treated me like I'd killed somebody. They wouldn't let my mother take me home. Mr. Dick was in his forties, and I was only ten. Maybe the police sergeant took one look at my breasts and limbs and figured my age from that, I don't know.

> Anyway, I guess they had me figured for having enticed this old goat into the whorehouse or something. All I know for sure is they threw me into a cell. My mother cried and screamed and pleaded, but they just put her out of the jailhouse and turned me over to a fat white matron. When she saw I was bleeding, she felt sorry for me and gave me a couple of glasses of milk. But nobody else did anything for me except give me filthy dirty looks and snicker to themselves.
>
> After a couple of days in a cell they dragged me into court. Mr. Dick got sentenced to five years. They sentenced me to a Catholic institution.[2]

Black men who commit incest, rape and other forms of sexual abuse against black girls have, to some extent, bought the stereotype surrounding black women's sexuality; either it's that or they just don't care. It is equally important to say, however, that as black women we do not help matters when at times, we also lose sight of who we are, and allow ourselves to internalise the negative assumptions about our sexuality. For example, we begin to think that, somehow, maybe the abuse really was our fault because we have these bodies that are tempting men. Some of us worry about bottoms which we may think are too big; or breasts which are too full. We begin to feel that we *must* be responsible for the failure of men who abuse us to control themselves.

It is equally important to point out that a great many black women do not require validation from white norms in order to see the beauty of our bodies. Many of us love, admire and are proud of the way we look. The stereotype, after all, is the problem of those who utilise it; we know who we are. That is not to say, however, that we are unaffected by it. And nowhere is this more pronounced than when it comes to incest and child sexual abuse.

Psychologist Gail Wyatt, who was the first researcher to design a large-scale community study to explore differences and similarities in the prevalence of and responses to child sexual abuse of Afro-American and white women found, in relation to Afro-American women and sexual abuse, that 'Afro-American women tended to seek more internal reasons, such as their physical development, as the cause for their victimization'.[3]

These comments from two black women survivors say much about our predicament and the feelings which present themselves:

> When I was first abused by my brother's friend, I didn't know what to do. My biggest fear was that my father would say I caused it. That's because we are taught that our sexuality should remain suppressed until we're married. Otherwise, it shouldn't be there, and if something happens, then we've asked for it.

> I remember being cursed by my mom all through adolescence and being told things like my bottom was too big . . . My sister got pregnant at 16. I remember she once came after me, because she thought I was after her boyfriend. She accused me of fucking my father the whole time. All they could think was that I'd done this thing – not that it had been done to me.

There is a line in a song by the hard rap group, 2 Live Crew, which goes: 'There's only one way to fuck a bitch.' 'Bitch' translated, means woman, more especially, a black woman. An article in the *Education Guardian* (18 February 1992) addressed this tendency amongst some practitioners of hard rap to sexually dehumanise women. It also looked at how women rappers were countering the sexism contained in some rap: 'The world of rap is user-unfriendly if you're female. At best, women are "bitches" or "hos", short for "whores". A lot of rap deals with the sexual and social denigration of women.'

It is important to say here that not all rap or rappers denigrate women. Many rap stars, for example M.C. Hammer, refuse to participate in promoting the hard rap, misogynist ideas found in the genre. In addition, some of the ideas found in rap music – anti-drug or pro-education messages – provide positive guidelines for young people. It is also worth noting that some young women rappers challenge the anti-female stereotypes found in the music. Britain's Tatiana Mais, aka Q-TEE, has said: 'It makes me want to write more raps, to be more forceful, to fight against what they're trying to portray. The worst of the images come from the influential United States, breeding ground of the worst of rap's bad boys – and girls.'[4] She adds, too, that there is support amongst rap fans and musicians for a crusade against such blatant misogynist attitudes.

The fact remains, however, that there is still a notable proportion of young black male rappers who see no problem in bopping to or making a buck from music which distorts the images of the mothers, sisters, aunts and grandmothers who cherished, nurtured and loved them. Where is the respect that is the least that is due them? Where is the gratitude? But most of all, where is the love that has been replaced by the verbal sexual abuse of black women?

In her essay, 'Sexism: An American Disease in Blackface', the late Audre Lorde discusses the gulf that has existed between black men and black women. She notes the view among some black men which speaks of a 'curious rage' brought on by the effects of exploitation of black people. 'Is this rage any more legitimate than the rage of Black women?' Lorde asks. 'And why are Black women supposed to absorb that male rage in silence?' The logical extension of such black male disrespect and anger towards black women is death. Lorde notes that this is exactly what did happen to Patricia Cowan, a young black woman who 'answered an ad in Detroit for a Black actress to audition in a play called *Hammer*. As she acted out an argument scene, watched by the playwright's brother and her four-year-old son, the Black male playwright picked up a sledgehammer and bludgeoned her to death.'[5]

By comparison, those of us who are sexually abused and debased are lucky. At least most of us, if indeed we are lucky, live to tell the tale. What is the reason for this debasement of the black woman and her sexuality? Why are our lives, our hopes, our aspirations not considered important? Why do the young rapping men who belong to the school of hard rap feel no shame or remorse for reducing their mothers, sisters, aunts and lovers, to body parts, embodied in pejorative slang? Why does the venting of black male rage so often involve denigration of or harm to the black woman, either sexually or otherwise?

Racism and sexuality

It is important to look at such abuse within a historical context. In an interesting film entitled *I Want Your Sex*, producer/director Yaba Badoe made the connection between racism and myth concerning black male and female sexuality.[6]

Her point of origin was slavery. Using a compelling series of interviews she shows how these myths have, over time, been perpetuated: myths concerning perceptions of black women *and* black men as possessions and curiosities. In the nineteenth century, for example, a black woman, Saartje Bartman, also known as the Hottentot Venus, was brought to England from South Africa by a Boer, and paraded around the country as an attraction because of the size of her buttocks. The eroticism attached to black women has also been a crucial component in moulding the myths and shaping perceptions. For example, in the 1920s Josephine Baker became the toast of Paris because of her suggestive and sexual dancing (Who can forget the banana dance?). More recent is the sculptured animal sexuality of singer Grace Jones which is said to have been deliberately engineered by her white male publicist.

These are inescapable manifestations of the 'perverse' curiosity about the African body. According to historian David Dabydeen, whites who participated in the rape (literally and otherwise) of African cultures wanted not just to undress black people but to subjugate them, and one of the ways in which this was done was through sexual conquest.[7]

Further evidence of this can be seen in the way that black women have been photographed anthropologically – naked, or with breasts bared. Academic Kobena Mercer has noted the fascination with the 'exotic other' which black people represent sexually to whites, but which is also viewed as threatening to the order of (white) society.[8]

Frantz Fanon described this double consciousness – this tendency for sexuality to underpin every facet of relations between black and white; a tendency which is often evident to black people in even the most cursory of encounters with white people:

> In relation to the Negro, everything takes place on the genital level . . . On the phenomenological level there would be a double reality observed. The Jew is feared because of his potential for acquisitiveness . . . As for the Negroes, they have tremendous sexual powers. What do you expect, with all the freedom they have in their jungles! They copulate at all times and in all places. They are really genital. They have so many children that they cannot even count them. Be careful, or they will flood us with little mulattoes.[9]

Part and parcel of the 'otherness' in relation to black people's sexuality is the equation of black as bad and white as good. Again, Fanon:

> The Negro is genital. Is this the whole story? Unfortunately

> not. The Negro is something else. Here again we find the Jew. He and I may be separated by the sexual question, but we have one point in common. Both of us stand for Evil. The black man more so, for the good reason that he is black. Is not whiteness in symbols always ascribed in French to Justice, Truth, Virginity? I knew an Antillean who said of another Antillean, 'His body is black, his language is black, his soul must be black too.' This logic is put into daily practice by the white man. The black man is the symbol of Evil and Ugliness.

Unfortunately for black women, and the sexually defined straitjacket within which we are placed, this logic is also put into practice by black people.

All of us possess, by virtue of the fact that we inhabit our physical beings, a body world. The European body world sets the standard by which all bodies are measured – and the European body is felt to confer whiteness, goodness, right.

For black people, since slavery and colonialism, the idea of a black body world is fraught with negative imagery – the bad black nigger who's just waiting for the chance to rape white womanhood or the promiscuous black whore who lacks morals and is therefore deserving of the misuse and abuse perpetrated against her by men – black and white.

Beryl Gilroy notes that, historically, black people have grappled with a body type which is regarded as inferior, and have, as a result, striven to achieve a body that is out of keeping with what is right for us as a people.[10] This tension has caused confusion for many black women – some hate their bodies, or at the very least feel, and have been taught to feel, uncomfortable with them. One black woman survivor described her feelings about her body like this:

> I did a 'Fat is a Feminist Issue' workshop. One of the images I had was that when I was slim, I could take my vagina – an

> exploding vagina – and splatter all the people in the room. Now, I feel my sexuality has been worked through and I've become less afraid of my body being an abuser's, just because it exists. I used to feel that my body was dangerous – like Medusa's. So that it [the incest] was all my fault for having the body. But now, I'm feeling that less and less.

Many black women who have been sexually abused internalise the negativeness until we can no longer relate to our innermost selves or to acknowledge our right to exist as who we are. When we reach this point we begin to take on, with frightening ease, the language and the sensibilities of our abusers. This is reflected in the language and the thoughts of one black woman incest survivor:

> The first boyfriend I had, I had sex with. I was still a virgin [despite incestuous experience]. That made me feel dirty. I used to be really into sex. If I felt a guy didn't want me for sex, then I felt I was no use to him. That's all I wanted from them and that's all I got.

This internalised negativeness has historically and in the present day been built upon and accepted by many black males in our communities. Eldridge Cleaver, for example, is in a sense, the literary predecessor of 2 Live Crew. This is an excerpt from his major work, *Soul on Ice*:

> To refine my technique, I started out by practising on black girls in the black ghetto, where the dark and vicious deeds are not seen as aberrations or deviations from the norm, but as part of the sufficiency of the evil of a day; and when I felt myself smooth enough, I crossed the tracks and sought out white prey.[11]

The casual manner in which sex with black women/girls is justified in pursuit of black male macho conquests brings into focus issues of race and gender, with considerably less importance attached to gender, and reinforces the idea of black women as sexual objects. The consequence of this is to make us invisible – and as unseen objects, it is an easy step to regard us as not worthy of being loved, cherished or respected.

Again, in *Soul on Ice*, in an essay entitled, 'The Allegory of the Black Eunuchs', one of Cleaver's characters describes his feelings about lovemaking with black women:

> You may not believe this . . . when I off a nigger bitch, I close my eyes and concentrate real hard, and pretty soon I get to believing that I'm riding one of them bucking blondes. I tell you the truth, that's the only way that I can bust my nuts with a black bitch, to close my eyes and pretend that she is Jezebel. If I was to look down and see a black bitch underneath me or if my hand happened to feel her nappy hair, that would be the end, it would be all over. I might as well get on up and split because I wouldn't be able to get anything down, even if I piled her all night long.

Apart from the obvious debasement through the language that he chose to use, Cleaver is clearly addressing the view held by some black males, that black women are second rate. Abuse of all kinds becomes much easier if you don't regard the victim as deserving of equal status or consideration. 'One tool of the Great-American-Double-Think,' writes Audre Lorde, 'is to blame the victim for victimization: Black people are said to invite lynching by not knowing our place; Black women are said to invite rape and murder and abuse by not being submissive enough, or by being too seductive, or too . . .'[12]

Pornography and prurience

Black women's sexuality is also affected by the images of us as whores/hot mamas/bitches consolidated by the blaxploitation films of the 1960s and 1970s. Set in the black, urban milieu, they combined violence and sex to create cardboard stereotypes of black men and women, and exploited the sexual mythology to the full. The hot, hip black chicks portrayed in films like *Cotton Comes to Harlem, Cleopatra Jones* and *Shaft*, served to shore up the image of the exotic, passionate black woman, who would do anything, and to whom you could do anything, as long as she was pacified with the prospect of a good lay. These images were created almost entirely by white writers, producers and directors.

A notable exception was the 1971 film, *Sweet Sweetback's Baadasssss Song*. Written, produced, directed, financed, scored and starred in by a black man, Melvin Van Peebles, it continued the strain of blaxploitation films, and in particular the sexual exploitation of black women, with its portrayal of a super black stud. When it came out, I was living in Los Angeles. The film premièred at the local black cinema, and the whole community turned out to hail it as a breakthrough. Interestingly, however, the breakthrough was only in terms of the black man – the black male filmmaker and the black male character who is allowed to vent his frustration at his oppression in white society. Nothing was said about the black woman's feelings about her oppression.

Pornography plays an important part in the imagery. Pornographic images of black women show us as picturesque, removed from self and deserving of – even asking for – enslavement. Historically, as I noted earlier, this goes back to the desire and ability of white men to abuse black women sexually, as a matter of right. Black women were chattel and property, and, as such, were consigned to accept the position that had been mapped out for them – to provide physical labour and sexual pleasure for white men.

Though all women are victimised by pornography, the treatment of black women is different. Alice Walker wrote about this difference in her essay, 'Coming Apart': 'The pornography industry's exploitation of the black woman's body is *qualitatively* different from that of the white woman. Where white women are depicted in pornography as objects, black women are depicted as animals; where white women are depicted at least as human beings, black women are depicted as shit.'[13]

In the 1980s, attempts by black male filmmakers to deal with black women's sexuality have also fallen wide of the mark. The premier example of this is Spike Lee's groundbreaking film, *She's Gotta Have It* (1986). Although the film sets out to take black women out of the realm of invisibility, it ends up making us more invisible because it reinforces those long-held sexual stereotypes.

The film's title character, Nola Darling, is presented as a liberated woman, for which we are to read, sexually liberated. Her main interest in life, as far as can be seen, is to be fucked by one of three male suitors who are the dominant people in her life. She has no control and no motive for being, except that of animal lust and pleasure. She can see no further than the sexual gratification she gets from her encounters with these men.

Nola, however, is not sexually liberated. She is not in control of her destiny, and her so-called liberation is grounded only in her relations with the men with whom she is involved – it is, in fact, *dependent* on their interpretations of it. Nola is so dependent, in fact, that she mutely accepts being raped by Jamie, one of her suitors, because her sexual needs are so great that she cannot or does not want (we are asked to believe) to distinguish between brutality and love.

Nola, in reality, is one-dimensional and emotionally scarred. Unlike the men in the film, she does not interact with or seem to be connected to a community. She has no being apart from the sexual one laid down for her. Her relationships with her women friends are thinly etched in, unlike the characters of the men in the film, whose sexuality is only one dimension of a varied, whole and connected person. There is no attempt to portray a similar closeness and intimacy between Nola and her friends, which would undeniably be the case in real-life relationships between black women. Nola, instead, is reduced to a 'pussy', and little else.

It is little wonder then that in real life, when black girls are sexually abused (by their fathers, uncles, brothers, grandfathers, friends of the family) given the onslaught of such media images – even those intended as progressive – that we internalise the trauma they induce as no more than what we can expect. What is more, many black men don't even know what we're talking about if we try to say, 'This hurts'. Many can't (or say they can't) understand what it is we're going on about when we say we don't want to be abused any more. Writer Michele Wallace has said that the reason why some black men internalise the myths has to do with the fact that 'being men . . . it didn't occur to them that they needed also to reject the gender as well as racist ideology. I guess they figured one out of two ain't bad.'[14]

Keeping up appearances – internalising the abuse

An indication of the effect all of this has on black women who have been victimised by incest can be gained from Diana Russell's ground-breaking study in 1986. One of the outgrowths of this study was a comparison of the effects of incestuous abuse reported by Afro-American and white American women. Although Russell found no statistically significant differences in the prevalence of incestuous abuse for Afro-American and white women, it was possible nevertheless to draw conclusions about the effects on the women as a result of their experiences. Among Russell's findings were the following:

> **Severity**
> Incestuous abuse of Afro-American incest victims was over three times more likely than incestuous abuse of white victims to be at the *very severe* level. (Experiences involving oral, anal or vaginal intercourse were considered *very severe* abuse, those involving genital fondling or attempted fondling, *severe abuse*, and more minor acts of sexual contact or attempted contact, *least severe* abuse [author's emphasis].)
>
> Whereas 56 per cent of the experiences reported by Afro-American incest victims involved some form of intercourse or attempted intercourse, the same was true of less than one-fifth (18 per cent) of the experiences reported by white incest victims.
>
> . . . Other factors that are unique to the life circumstances of Afro-American women in this culture may also play a part in their reporting more trauma as a result of incestuous abuse than White women. For example, the trauma of incestuous abuse may be compounded by the trauma of being born and raised as an Afro-American female in a racist and sexist culture.[15]

Ain't *that* the truth! The reality for black women who have been sexually abused as children is, on the one hand, that of trying to maintain some kind of equilibrium in their lives, all the while carrying round their terrible secrets; while on the other, being *expected* by our families and our communities to carry on as if nothing had happened.

That many of us have been able to do so is a tribute to our strength and determination to try and put the trauma behind us. In a very real sense, though, we are victims of our success. We have become too good at keeping quiet, at absorbing it, at moving beyond it, at achieving in spite of it. But it is only qualified success. Qualified, because in the long run it only serves to reinforce the idea that abusive behaviour does not *have* to change, because there is no mandate for it to do so. The following comments from a 1991 international black women's conference workshop on women and sexual abuse bears this out:

– One woman reported that in her Panamanian community a 15-year-old girl who was being abused by her father was told by the family: 'It's better for everybody if you go with him.'

– In some African societies, a woman does not leave her husband if he abuses her daughter, in part because it reduces the girl's chances for marriage. Instead the daughter undergoes a cleansing ceremony.

– Someone else noted that, 'We need to widen the definition of abuse because in some societies, a 40-year-old man can rape a 12-year-old girl and the girl gets blamed. In some African societies, men of any age can marry girl children, and that's also abuse.'

– One woman who was raped, and became pregnant as a result, couldn't tell her family or anyone in her community, and left the town where she lived. She has a 15-year-old daughter. As black women, we don't tell about the abuse which happens to us. We keep it in – the guilt and the hurt – because of the way society thinks about our sexuality.

– Comment from a young black woman who had been a victim of rape: 'Maybe it was my fault. Maybe I shouldn't have been there.'

Precisely because we are vulnerable – as black people, as women – there is a great reluctance to divulge painful information (and incest probably ranks as one of the most painful). We worry that it will rebound on us as a community and reinforce long-held stereotypes about black people and how we behave. Counsellor Pat Agana, who works with women and children who have been sexually abused, has outlined the mind-set that takes place for the abused black child:

> Addressing child sexual assault, as with child abuse, means for us for to address racism.

When Africans were first enslaved it was necessary for Europeans to evolve a philosophy of justification. In the process well over 75 million Africans were left at the bottom of the sea. These basic assumptions inform this society's interaction with us to this very day. Ideas which have become enshrined in this country's culture:

> we are not quite human;
> we are highly sexual beings; we know nothing about parenting;
> we have no language, no culture, no traditions;
> being Black we are synonymous with evil;
> we are aggressive;
> we know * * * * *
> we are assumed to be physical not intellectual

... The abused child feels responsible for what has taken place. The abused child feels dirty, the abused child feels alone, the abused child feels angry, the abused child feels negative about themself [*sic*] and all these feelings feed into the impact. An African child who has been sexually abused can confuse this whole experience with what it is to be an African, the outcome is very often a compounded self hate.[16]

Women loving women

Years passed with my 'secret' locked safely away. I got on with my life as best I could, worked hard at various dead-end jobs, and eventually gave up sleeping with men. I had always been close to women, at least those outside my family, and had always loved my women friends a lot.

Black women who sexually love other women – lesbians – are considered the lowest of the low by too many in black communities. They are almost universally – within their communities – singled out for hostility, ridicule and contempt. The reasons for this are complex and have their roots in perceptions of black male sexuality and the homophobia which is, for some, a result of it.

Audre Lorde wrote about this juxtaposition of racism and sexism, as it impinges on the sexuality of black women who love other women, in her book of essays, *Sister Outsider*:

> Today, the red herring of lesbian-baiting is being used in the Black community to obscure the true face of racism/sexism. Black women sharing close ties with each other, politically or emotionally, are not the enemies of Black men. Too frequently, however, some Black men attempt to rule by fear those Black women who are more ally than enemy.
>
> All too often the message comes loud and clear to Black women from Black men: 'I am the only prize worth having and there aren't too many of me, and remember, I can always go elsewhere. So if you want me, you'd better stay in your place which is away from one another, or I will call you "lesbian" and wipe you out.'[17]

Lorde goes on to recount how in the late 1970s 'rule by terror' was instituted against Black women who attempted to come together around women's concerns on the campus of a New York State college. Threats of violence and a general climate of intimidation resulted in some black women being beaten and raped.

'Instead of keeping our attentions focused upon our real needs, enormous energy is being wasted in the Black community today in anti-lesbian hysteria,' writes Lorde.

> Yet women-identified women – those who sought their own destinies and attempted to execute them in the absence of male support – have been around in all of our communities for a long time . . . for example, the unmarried aunt, childless or otherwise, whose home and resources were often a familiar figure in many of our childhoods. And within the homes of our Black communities today, it is not the Black lesbian who is battering and raping our underage girl-children out of displaced and sickening frustration.

Many black lesbians are survivors of incest and other forms of child sexual abuse. Many are not. Nor do all survivors of incest become lesbians because of it. I have spoken to a number of black women who are lesbians and who survived incest. Though no one I spoke with felt they were lesbian because of their experiences of incest, many raised the issue of an inability to trust men as a contributing factor. I also spoke with women who lacked trust in men, who were not lesbians.

> The last guy I went out with used to beat me up. I started to feel that I didn't want to be with him or with any man. And I started to have feelings for women. I've always had feelings for women . . . I don't hate men, but I just do not trust them. If there's a man in the room, I get very nervous and self-conscious. I feel exposed. I feel that I have to feel sexual towards him and that if he gives me compliments I must throw myself at his feet. I have male friends; but they're gentle and un-macho.

Being victimised by incest does not necessarily make you change your sexuality. What it does do, however, is create the necessity for examining what may be long-held beliefs and practices concerning ideas of how we should be as black women. Those ideas may have to do with our feelings about being sexually abused as little girls; or they may be about opening our hearts, minds and bodies to the joys of loving women.

It is inescapable that we should be the determiners of our own sexuality. Yet often for a black woman who has been victimised by incest, and who comes out as a lesbian, there exist the twin realities of rejection as a survivor, in the sense that she is neglected and invisible, and as a lesbian, because she is not.

> I wasn't intending to come out as a lesbian at the time. I

> was just telling ——— where to go. I told my dad I didn't want men. He said: 'You're one of those funny women. Your mother's not going to like this.' . . . My mother sat in the dark for two weeks and cried. She wouldn't touch me or eat food that I'd prepared, or come near me. She never touched me for ten years.

The rejection, by their families and communities, of black women who are lesbian compounds the pain for those who are also survivors. They are said to be anti-men. In some instances that is the case; in others, it is not. (In fact, many women who survive incest, myself included, went on to have creditable relationships with our fathers. Trust is not so easily won back, however.)

Whether some black women choose to love other women sexually is not the issue. What *is* important is that black communities examine their own homophobic attitudes, without creating scapegoats and inflicting further pain on those already having to withstand abusive attitudes within those communities. A statement which came out of a workshop on lesbianism at a conference on feminist practice and child sexual abuse spoke to this issue:

'We do not reject the premise that our past experiences and herstory influence our present. However, this is also true of heterosexuals who never ask themselves why they are heterosexuals. Underlying the premise is that we are lesbians only because we had a bad experience with men and if only we could somehow resolve our difficulties with men, we will no longer be lesbians. This view is held by both men and women heterosexuals, and is rejected by us.'[18]

> I still entertain the fantasy of being heterosexual. I wish I could remove this capacity within me to love women in this way. I'd be much happier. But I can't cope with the dishonesty. I've been on sexual binges when I went out and slept with men and had sex, and tried to convince myself

that I could be normal. I've got to the stage in my life now where I realise it's bullshit.

I used to cry all the time. I know that I could be happy if it was legal to be a lesbian. I could carry this baggage [of the abuse] but it would be history – it wouldn't bother me. To me, the most natural thing in the world is to love another woman. I don't feel dirty or sordid. I can't accept the church's argument that it is wrong. I can't imagine how loving someone can be wrong.

The politics of telling – what's the big deal?

The minefield surrounding black women's sexuality leaves us open and vulnerable to being attacked – verbally and physically; or at the very least, to risk being severely misinterpreted.

In many respects black women are expected to be *Sistahs*. That translates into standing behind our *Brothers*. Standing behind our brothers takes many forms. It can mean that we are expected to acquiesce to sexual stimulation by our fathers, brothers, uncles, and friends of the family. It can mean that we are expected to 'understand' about oppressive acts in the name of the Brothers having their space. It can mean, and has meant, that we are expected to keep quiet about the injustice of incest, rape and other sexual crimes.

I feel we have a measure of responsibility within this. As black women, we are all too painfully aware of the injustices that are perpetuated against communities of colour. We know what it will mean, for example for a Brother if we report a crime of rape or incest. Every time it occurs we are faced with having to weigh the consequences to us *and* to our community. It was a consideration in my own case, and I am by no means unusual. You wonder: is it worth exposing our communities and our men to further harassment? Will we be believed by those within and without? Will it reinforce long-entrenched prejudices about what we are like as black people sexually? What good will it do; after all, it's a bit like closing the barn door after the horse has escaped, no?

By telling, blowing the whistle, shooting off our mouths, we run the risk of alienating ourselves across the spectrum in our communities. Will the good *Sistahs* in the Church believe we were totally innocent of blame in spreading our legs for our daddies? Will *we* believe it? Will our mothers regard us as grown women who are rivalling them for the affections and lovemaking of their menfolk? Will our blood *Sistahs* and Brothers believe we are totally without blame?

And if we *are* believed, will there be any amongst our community who will thank us for betraying the community to the wider world? Will our fathers, brothers, uncles, friends of the family feel betrayed that we did not accept their attentions in the spirit they may have been offered – to educate us; to make us feel loved; to make our men feel loved?

Will we be said, once again, to be guilty of deferring to the white man in an attempt to obstruct, yet again, the Brothers' progress? Will we be ostracised as Judas *Sistahs*, who could not accept our fate and be content to make the most of physical, sexual and emotional misuse?

Child sexual abuse is the misuse of power by an individual (usually male) against a child. Whether the child is black or white, it does harm. If the child *is* black, however, it does particular harm because of the added dimension of race. When a white child is sexually abused, they think they are bad and dirty. When a black child, especially a girl child, is abused, she thinks she is bad, dirty and an affront to the race, both in sexual terms and in terms of being black and female. She thinks too, of the message it will send to white society if she tells.

I felt an outcast because I was different – I was mixed race

> and nobody seemed to understand because there were not many mixed race children at my school. I was a different religion. I was a Muslim and lots of other children were Christian. I felt I was strange in some way.

There is a strong tendency amongst abused black girls/ women not to tell and not to discuss it. The underlying reasons for this attitude have to do with feelings of vulnerability centred around race and sex. Why tell, when there are so many negative stereotypes associated with being black anyway? Why tell, because it's just going to mean that we confirm their worst expectations of black people as sexual animals? Why tell and bring shame on to the family, the community? Why tell when we may just as likely be accused of colluding with the act as not?

> You hear all this [negative] stuff on telly about black people, black youths; and I take it all on board. I feel responsible. I went through a stage where I felt ashamed to be black. I feel there is a lot of anti-black feeling, even in the black community. For example, you sometimes hear black people describing themselves as rubber lips.

Too often, as a result, we succumb. We lose sight of who we should also be taking care of – ourselves, for a change. We bury our hopes, wishes, needs, under the many layers of that old chestnut called Expectations. People say to us: 'What are you making such a big deal for?' Or they say: 'You're basically OK, why make a fuss?' We listen, and we believe that really we aren't supposed to make a fuss. 'Where is our anger?' asked one participant at a black women's conference on child sexual abuse. Where indeed? Why do we allow our bodies and our psyches to be fucked over in the name of not letting the race, the community down? Are *we* not the community? Or are we only *Sistahs* if we keep our mouths shut about the abuse which is perpetrated against us? Where are the voices within our communities which urge us not to remain silent – which say it's not OK that as little girl children we had to spread our legs, and then were expected to keep quiet about it, because it happens all the time and really is no big deal?

The answer is that those voices must come from within us – black women who have survived incest. But we owe it to ourselves and our communities to do more than survive; we must thrive, if our communities are to thrive as well. Therefore, we must force the issue. We must confront the stereotypes which say that because we are black and female we can handle the pain and the ripping apart that childhood abuse causes.

We must point out that black girls should not have to grow up with behavioural and physical problems that manifest themselves through explicit sexual play, toilet problems, withdrawal, failure to thrive, bedwetting, sleep problems, fear and mistrust of adults, low self-esteem and actively entertaining feelings of suicide, all of which can directly result from having been sexually abused.

We must move away from making and accepting the excuses for the abuse. Excuses such as: 'He was drunk and probably didn't mean it', or, 'He didn't abuse her because she was already sexually active.' It has been estimated that 85 per cent of abuse is done by people we know, love and trust, and ought to feel safe with. Yet, as black women who have been abused we do not feel safe. We do not yet feel we can challenge the stereotypes which our own people hold for fear of raining down further indictments upon ourselves and upon our communities. We do not feel safe enough to say: 'Enough!'

In interviewing women for this book, I talked to many who were reluctant to discuss the issue, but who readily agreed it should be dealt with by our communities. 'You are very brave,' they said, 'and I'm glad you're doing it.'

I am not brave. I am tired, though, of letting all this stuff go unchallenged. I am not a sexual animal, nor have I ever been promiscuous. In fact, what happened between my father and myself had the opposite effect on me. It meant that I was afraid of relationships with men for many years. I can remember once, when I was about 18 or 19, being positively shocked to see my neighbour (who had a reputation for being a 'fast' girl) kissing a boy. Despite my experience of incest, I had never experienced anyone kissing in such a passionate way before, except on television; in real life, it gave me quite a fright.

In part, my fears had to do with worry that the incest would somehow become apparent to anyone I became close to. In part, to do with the fact that I might not be thought to be a good girl, and I, like many of us, was raised to be a good girl.

Fears about the stigma of shame that would descend on the rest of the family if the terrible secret ever came out were also uppermost in my mind. I was afraid, too, that the physical pleasure which, if I am honest, I have to admit was part of it, meant that if I looked too closely at myself and the incest, I would somehow find that the stereotype of loose sexual morality might after all apply to me. I know, of course, that it does not.

Reclaiming the anger

As black women, we must reclaim our anger and speak out about sexual abuse within our communities because, quite simply, it is a big deal. In that way we can reclaim the power that has been denied us. As black women, we must make our anger known so that those who would abuse us, and those who fail to challenge such abuse, will know – whether that abuse is blatant, as with sexual abuse; or the more subtle kind, involving a failure to challenge stereotypes – that we will not continue to suffer in silence.

Many of us are still confused as to why sexual abuse had to happen to us. One woman with whom I spoke still felt very real pain many years after the incidence of her abuse by a friend of the family. Hers was a struggle, full of anger and bewilderment, which characterised a battle being waged within herself (when we met, it was by no means a certainty that it was a battle she would win) to come to grips with why. For her, and for all of us, that struggle goes on, to greater or lesser degrees, in an effort to try and make some sense (if sense there is to be made of it) of why it happened. Was there an invisible sign on us that said, 'Black girl – free and easy? I'm sexually hot stuff. I'm available.' I think not. More than likely, what we were actually projecting was our need to be loved and cherished in an appropriate and non-hurtful way. The only crime for many of us was in not knowing how to articulate that need.

'Black women's literature is full of the pain of frequent assault,' said Audre Lorde, 'not only by a racist patriarchy, but also by Black men. Yet the necessity for, and history of, shared battles have made us, Black women, particularly vulnerable to the false accusation that anti-sexist is anti-Black. Meanwhile, womanhating as a recourse of the powerless is sapping strength from Black communities, and our very lives. Rape is on the increase, reported and unreported, and rape is not aggressive sexuality, it is sexualized aggression. As Kalamu ya Salaam, a Black male writer points out, "As long as male domination exists, rape will exist. Only women revolting and men made conscious of their responsibility to fight sexism can collectively stop rape."'[19]

Child abuse counsellor Pat Agana points out:

> The fact is that rape and sexual assault of children exist in our communities amongst our African peoples . . . It

> is here in our midst. Many of us . . . know individuals, directly or indirectly, who under a guise of righteousness have abused the respect of women, men and children. People often do not expose these people for fear, sheer embarrassment or pain. But our silence gives them too much power and undermines the things that we are working for. They also stand as misrepresentations of what African manhood is about.
>
> Our task is not to run from the existence of child sexual abuse, but to accept that it is a reality and thus listen and investigate information that children bring to us. I am advocating a conscious taking of responsibility for the welfare of our children by both men and women, whether we are the ones who gave birth to them or not. Those adults who commit these crimes against the community need help or are consciously involved in a mission of self destruction. Either way they have to be exposed and made to take responsibility for their actions.
>
> In the last 20 years, I have known of men, men who are known to many of us here, men who have and continue to rape and physically abuse women, men who have and continue to molest children. Women and children who are alone in their suffering. Yet they have been sheltered in our midst because we have not the systems in place to address the moral and spiritual health of our community. Very often the individuals responsible are the most well read and spout the most rhetoric. Political consciousness then is obviously not enought to safeguard a whole human being.[20]

My argument is that, as a people, we *do* have the moral and spiritual capacity to safeguard the soul and the sexuality of our female children. What is missing, often, is the will to act upon that capacity. For some reason, as black people, it is hard for us to acknowledge, and therefore do something about, the harm that sexual abuse does to our girls and subsequently our women. This failure to respond is due in large part to a refusal (perhaps to an inability, I don't know) to grasp the reality of black women's sexuality. That reality consists of nurture and care, as well as sex. We are not body parts, but whole, human women, with a helluva lot to give. Without such an acknowledgement, incest and CSA will remain and grow as a problem for black girls and black women; but also, in the long run, for black boys and men.

For myself, as a black woman who was abused as a child; who for years felt it was my fault in some way – because I didn't say no; because it must have been something in me; because, because, because . . . I am no longer willing to bear that cross of guilt or self-blame. Whatever my father's needs were sexually or emotionally, he should not have used my body to satisfy them. It was a boundary that should not have been crossed. There are no arguments which can convince me that this was the way things should have been.

The black woman's revolution then, must be fought on many fronts if it is to bring about a fundamental shift of attitudes regarding our sexuality. It must, however, begin with ourselves. It is important that we accept the beauty of our bodies, and that we teach our daughters to do so. We must also instil into them the crucial information that they do not have to accept unwanted advances – including inappropriate kissing, touching, feeling or cuddling from male relatives or friends of the family. We must also teach our sons about the beauty that is represented by the bodies of their mothers, grandmothers, aunts and sisters. We must make them understand that those bodies are to be cherished, not violated; adored, not invaded; protected, not abused.

The price we pay for remaining silent about incest and other sexual abuse is to internalise the pain and the negative feelings about ourselves – as survivors, as people. Instead of challenging it, some of us try to deny the pain by embracing it. We buy the notion that we are meant to be strong enough to put the experience behind us, and many of us do, until that day arrives when a smell, a sight, a sound, a look is enough to precipitate a crack. A crack that is made worse because it is not founded on what *we* know to be true about ourselves, but on what others would have us believe about ourselves.

We ought to listen – and would be better served by listening – more to our inner selves. We should be more attuned to our own instincts – unclouded by stereotypical perceptions or expectations. We should take what women like Toni Morrison have to say more to heart:

> When you really look at the stereotypes of Black women the worst you can say about them, that is once you disregard the vocabulary and the dirty words and deal with the substance of what is being said, is quite complimentary. Think about it. What is being said is that Black women are wonderful mothers and nurturers (mammies), that we are sexually at home in our bodies (oversexed), and that we are self-sufficient and tough (henpecking and overbearing). And isn't that exactly what *every* woman wants to be: loving and nurturing, sexually at home in her body, competent and strong?[21]

CHAPTER 4

Love, comfort and abuse

Some instances of incest represent a fine line between the giving and receiving of love and comfort, and the perpetration of abuse. At times, it is difficult for survivors either to recognise or to come to terms with the fact that the boundary has been crossed. The blurring of this line often unleashes emotions (or, conversely keeps them hidden) that many survivors find it impossible to deal with. Questions which may revolve around feeling sexual excitement, while simultaneously feeling uncomfortable with the hugs and touches. Questions about whether we are bad people are never far from the surface for some of us; as are feelings of guilt.

It is very hard to work through all of the feelings that are swirling around within us. When we do attempt it as survivors, we make the tacit decision to uncover truths about ourselves which may sometimes be overwhelmingly painful. We may be fearful of what we will find. We may be repulsed by it. We may reject it. But we ought at least to try and face it. That is my guiding principle in this chapter.

I have spoken with many women in an attempt to go beyond my own experience for the purpose of relating the feelings which black women have about their incest. Not everyone wanted their stories included. One of the most decisive moments for me in constructing what I would say came from one of my meetings with a woman who did not want to be formally interviewed, but who did want the point to be made that, in her own case, the incest was 'not always one-sided'.

She talked briefly about her incestuous experience with an uncle: 'Sometimes,' she said, 'I went to look for *him*.' Once she'd said it, it was if a great weight had lifted for her. She visibly relaxed and anxiously searched my face for signs of disapproval. She found none. And we realised that we had crossed a boundary of a different sort – one which would eventually free us from the guilt we carried about our experiences. It was a revelation and a relief, for both of us, to hear those dreaded thoughts voiced. For me, it marked the lifting of the final taboo about the incest.

Though I never forgot my abuse, as many women do, I also never really permitted myself a true exploration of all my feelings surrounding it. The other side of the coin, for me, as a twelve-year-old with an awakening sexuality, was that the experience with my father was, at times, sexually pleasurable; as well as comforting. It is a very hard admission to make if you believe and argue, as I do, that the incest was wrong, and should never have happened – not to me, not to any of the young black girls who underwent and still undergo sexual intimacy with fathers, uncles, brothers, grandfathers who don't hold the boundaries.

As I said earlier, my father's and my relationship was not brutal or threatening. He was very gentle and I liked the cuddles he gave me. I liked being close enough to smell his aftershave and the intimacy of snuggling up against his chest. It made me feel special, loved, wanted, needed. The price I have had to pay for accepting those cuddles is thirty-odd years of consummate guilt, self-doubt and blame. It is much too high a price.

Before I go any further, I must point out that many women involved in incestuous relationships do not share these memories of their abuse. For some, there was no aspect of it which could even remotely be considered loving, of which the following are examples:

> My father was my abuser. My parents were Jamaican. We lived in the rural areas of Jamaica until the early 50s, when first my father and then my mother left to come to England.
>
> My father had three other children before he married my mother. Then, they had me and three more children – seven altogether. I was the sixth child. I have one sister and five brothers.
>
> Both my parents were manual workers. We weren't an affectionate family. It was just the opposite – we used to kiss mum goodbye, but it was more of a duty.
>
> The abuse started when I was five. My father usually abused me when he put me to bed or when my mother went out. It started with penetration. It ended when I was 13. I wasn't able to tell my mother. She died when I was 10.
>
> All of the others [brothers and sisters] were born in Jamaica. When I was nine or 10, one of my brothers (who was four years older than me) started abusing me. He said it was because he loved me. He never threatened me. I was the special one – I was his favourite. My sister was too, but she wasn't abused.
>
> It almost worked on me. There were a lot of things we didn't have, and towards the end, it was; 'If you do this, you'll get x or y.' Plus these were things that I needed.
>
> I started to tell when I was 10. I had started to say to my father: 'You're not supposed to do this – it's wrong.' He would say: 'Your mother's not here, so she doesn't know.' It took three years for him to stop. After that, there was another two years when he still harassed me – until I was 16. He'd come over and say: 'Don't you want to come to bed with me?'
>
> I used to do anything to get out of the house. I didn't

> enjoy it. Most of the time I felt sick and couldn't get clean enough.

The experiences of one woman incest survivor point to the other extreme – a total absence of a loving experience, with the abuse being carried out solely in a brutal and dehumanising way:

> My abuse happened when I was a toddler. There was penetration when I was seven. My father was the abuser. It continued until I was 16 or 17. When it came out through social services, and it was proved, I was made a ward of the court.
>
> My mom and dad had a bad marriage. My dad was violent. I had a strict upbringing. I was not allowed to talk to other people. My dad picked me up from and took me to school. He stamped it in my head that I could never talk about it to anybody. He said it could break up the family and he could go to prison. And he said he would get me anyway, when he came out.
>
> My mother knew what was going on. But she was a weak person. He kicked hell out of her; tortured her. She couldn't speak English. She knew from when I was 11, when she caught my dad having sex with me. She blamed both of us. But I got her main anger.
>
> He told her that if she told he would kill her. He lived in the house with his third wife; and still had my mom in the house, as a cleaner. He also had sex with her when he wanted to.
>
> I tried to kill myself twice – when I was 14 and 15. His third wife wanted me to call her mother. I refused. She was a year or two younger than me. My dad had sex with me in front of her. I took an overdose. I was sent to see a psychiatrist.
>
> My case went to the Old Bailey. But there was no corroboration, so he walked out of court smiling.

None among us would be able to characterise this as anything other than what it was – a blatant and brutal abuse of power, sexual and otherwise. This is the other extreme. Between this and the occurrence of less overtly threatening relationships are a multitude of emotions, feelings and thoughts which need to be honestly examined.

What comfort is there now, for example, for those of us who did feel comforted, even loved as a result of our incestuous experiences? Yes, it *is* right that we hold the men responsible for failing to rein in their sexual libido, but the picture tends to become a bit blurred when it comes to looking at the victim as a participant. If a child derives physical pleasure, then is it correct to say it was abuse? 'I didn't think of it as abuse,' said one survivor. 'It was just that my mother stopped touching us.' Undeniably, many women who have experienced incest did not find it as horrific as the above two examples.

Psychotherapist Sonia Francis says, 'I almost feel that if people say: "I didn't think it was abuse," then maybe it wasn't abuse, because if you don't think it was, maybe it wasn't.' She admits, however, that, 'It gets very complicated, because the feelings [of survivors] are often connected with issues about loss – of a caring, nurturing parent – either a father or a mother – who is not there as a result of migration.'[1] (This idea of 'not being there' could likewise be understood to mean being there physically but not emotionally.)

Francis points out that everyone wants the closeness and the feeling of being wanted or special. 'They can remember that, but as well as the memory of the closeness and of being special, there is the anger and frustration; and an awareness that the sexual aspect was wrong. I won't let anybody deny there was some of that,' she adds. 'Parental figures take on a godlike state. They tell you what's good and what's bad. The problem is that the abusing parent doesn't hold his boundary, and allows the child to engage in something the child should not be engaging in. There is nearly always an awareness in children, however, that it is wrong.'

'But I took the sweets'

The dilemma which incest victims/survivors face in accounting for their own actions within the context of the experience is considerable. On the one hand, we are told that we are not to blame for what happened: this is the currently held view in mainstream discussion. Within the context of the black community we are told nothing, except to forget it.

On the other hand, despite the fact that our grown-up selves can rationalise that it is not our fault; that we were children; powerless and in awe of our parents; we are nevertheless left with the nagging doubt that after all, maybe it *was* our fault. The words of one child whom a black social worker had attempted to console following her abuse, with the explanation that the sexual intimacy with her abuser was not her fault, sums it up: 'But miss,' she said, 'I took the sweets.'

I fear this business of taking the sweets is one which – although we can admit to ourselves on an intellectual level that it was not our fault – takes a lot longer for that knowledge to sink in on a gut level. In part, this is due to the opinion of many in black and white communities that yes, indeed, we did take the sweets; in part it is due to our own inability to truly reconcile ourselves to the very real ideas concerning power and dominance. Writing in the *New York Times Magazine* (21 October 1990) Carol Lynn Mithers notes:

> Children's typical response to being sexually abused, research had begun to show, was a very distinctive one. They could not blame the abusive parent or see him as evil, for that was too psychologically threatening for a dependent

> child. Telling someone was almost equally unthinkable, for to tell would be to destroy the family. Since victimized children felt helpless to stop the abuse, most simply found a way to accommodate it. They pretended it wasn't happening. They shut down all their feelings. They blamed themselves.

In her book, *Incest, Fact & Myth,* Sarah Nelson refers to some of the [male] thinking surrounding the issue of female guilt and blame: 'In his review of the incest literature, Henderson notes a major finding, "Incestuous daughters are generally felt to encourage their fathers' sexual advances, or at least to refrain from discouraging them."' She goes on to quote two child psychiatrists at an Edinburgh incest seminar:

> A great deal of clinical practice suggests kids from 2–3 years have strong desires of an incestuous nature . . . [in] interviewing they know what sex is, they understand . . . Active steps are taken to maintain and initiate sex relationships with adults . . . children are very sexy and at times may choose to be . . . the commonness of incest may come back to the sexiness of children.[2]

Freud

No discussion about incest would be complete without Freud, who of course had much to say on the subject. I make no attempt to include a definitive account of his views, but it is important to look at some of the issues he raised in his attempts to understand and explain the sexual abuse many of his female clients underwent as children.

Freud did not write with black women in mind. Black women in common with white women, however, are still having to deal with the legacy of Freud's misogynist views. It is instructive to go back to Freud to try to gain a broader understanding of how the scenario of 'I took the sweets' fits into attempts to blame children, particularly female children, for the boundary-crossing engaged in by their fathers.

Florence Rush, in *The Best Kept Secret,* includes an excellent essay on Freud and his intentions. In 'A Freudian Cover-up', she refers to Freud's presentation, in 1905, of his theory on infant sexuality: 'He informed a society still deep in Victorian prudery that very small children had strong erotic drives. His theory shocked middle-class sensibilities at first, but eventually this same middle-class society came to find Freud to be quite right.'[3]

Rush points to the 'almost universal acceptance' today of the idea that children have erogenous zones and sexual feelings. But she notes that Freud, in concentrating on the psychosocial aspects of human development, gave little attention to other infantile endowments: 'He chose not to notice, for instance, that just as children are sexually aware, so are all their other faculties intact, and therefore they know when they have been humiliated and exploited.'

Freud's theories were based on his treatment, in psychoanalysis, of large numbers of nineteenth-century middle-class women, who were suffering from what was called hysteria (a common female ailment of that era). Many of the women who came to Freud, indeed most, reported sexual abuse by their fathers. At first Freud believed these women and drew a connection between the sexual abuse and the hysteria with which they presented.

Rush notes, however: 'But exposure to repeated and persistent incrimination of fathers by his patients made him uneasy, and never quite comfortable with the seduction theory; he mentioned it publicly only in the year 1896 and not again until much later (1933), when he was able to reassign the abuse to female fantasy and disavow it as erroneous.' Rush notes that although Freud never mentioned the theory in public, he did continue to collect data, and in private letters to his friend Wilhelm Fleiss held to the belief that female children were seduced by their fathers on a broad scale, and that this accounted for the neuroses suffered by his patients.

According to Rush, Freud went on to formulate the Oedipus complex: 'the theory of innate erotic attraction of children to parents of the opposite sex, and . . . gave us the "libido theory", or depiction of sexual energy as a vital life force'. This theory, which took its name from the Greek experience of Oedipus, who killed his father and married his mother (unknowingly), was derived from Freud's own self-analysis. He examined his own neurosis, which became apparent at the death of his father, and uncovered his own feelings of erotic love towards his mother, and jealousy of his father.

Rush notes that:

> Freud freely applied his particular personal discovery to everybody, to all cultures, and to females as well as males . . . so, as the son loved the mother and hated the father, so did the daughter love the father and hate the mother, he said. But he found the daughter's desire and need for the father so much more powerful than that of the son for his mother *that the daughter's wish to be seduced found its fulfillment in fantasy and fictitious seduction stories* [Rush's emphasis].

Thus, in a deft stroke of intellectual gymnastics, Freud was able to reassign responsibility for the sexual abuse from the fathers, where it belonged, to the female children, where it has remained. What this means for those of us who are black and have been abused is that we have a double oppression with which to contend – that imposed by stereotypical views concerning our sexuality in the first place, superimposed with male views, expanded upon by Freud, the Father of Psychoanalysis.

So it is little girls who are at fault, for desiring their fathers; and black little girls more so, because of their unchecked sexuality. The end result is that it is often very difficult for us to untangle the guilt and deep-down feelings that we *are* as much to blame. This view, by and large, frames our view of the abuse.

As a consequence, many of us find it hard to work at shifting the opinion which states that we must have wanted it, initiated it at times, even; because, after all, we did take the sweets, did we not? There are a number of things it is important for us as black women to look at. This is so for any woman really, who has been abused. But for black women in particular, because we have been taught that we can and ought to shoulder more than our share of the burden – any burden, without complaint – that we are, in effect, 'the mules of the world'.

To try to understand why, within the context of incest and CSA, we do this, as survivors we need to examine: (1) any sense of pleasure we may or may not have derived from the abuse; (2) the guilt associated with it; and (3) our coping mechanisms for resolving that guilt.

Guilty pleasure

After finally being able to broach, in my heart of hearts, the pleasurable aspect of the incest with my father, I felt, in equal proportions, great floods of relief and horror that I could be so bold and so bad. I was glad finally to be able to admit to myself outright the worst thing that I knew about myself – that I had experienced enjoyment from a wicked act, an act I knew to be wrong and (so I thought) uncommon. Yet I felt afraid at what finally making this revelation would mean in terms of my own assessment (as well as other people's) of my worth as a human being; and how it would govern my ability to accuse.

I think I always knew, however, that I could never get away from the fact that I had at times willingly participated.

Knew that if I were ever to come to terms, really come to terms with it in my own head, it would have to be said to myself. It would have to be squarely faced – leaving me with no illusions about the act or my part in it.

What then? Well, on one level – the intellectual one – I was fine about it. I understand the arguments that say it's not my fault, or that my father abused his power over me as an adult to a child. I do understand all of that and I believe it. But on another level it is a helluva thing to have to come to terms with; an admission that you liked some of those things your dad did with you – that though in many ways it was confusing, and left you with a lot of contradictions, there were moments when it was nice.

I had to shake off the nagging feeling that I had no right to bring it all up again – to be the accuser, because of that fact. I still grapple with whether or not I am engaging in hypocrisy of the first order by making my father the baddie in the whole thing, when the fact of my enjoyment is inescapable. Trying to answer that question is a big hurdle for many of us to get over – even though we may be aware of it intellectually.

It's important, however, to unpack that pleasure, to look at it more closely to see what kind of animal it was. The closeness, that feeling of being able to touch someone in a tender way, was, for me anyway, a big part of it. If the only time you got cuddles was when your dad said come and sit on my lap, then that's what you did. It is not bad to want cuddles or to be close to someone. It's – well, it's pleasurable. What is wrong is to infer from our simple enjoyment of being close that we also enjoyed the abuse.

Pat Agana notes that every child is born willing to interact with his or her environment. Every child is born willing to trust and to learn.[4] That is the given. Children's lives are based on their experiences, and it is the learning which those experiences bring that conditions their automatic responses to the world around them.

Knowledge that is gained through painful or puzzling experiences is taken into our psyches, just like that gained through positive experiences. It all goes to make up what then becomes our own particular normality. This learned behaviour may be anything from mastering French to participation in sexual abuse in the middle of the afternoon. The thing to remember is that it is *learned* behaviour.

For many people (though not all), sex is physically pleasurable. But sex is not love or affection. Reduced to basics, it is the satisfaction of a biological urge. When looking at sex and sexual abuse, it is important to note that many women who have been abused were faced with taking love as they found it – regarding and coming to equate sexual abuse with love. It came about because many of us were also faced with men who also did not know the difference and who were, to some extent, victims of their own emotional limitations.

> My own feeling used to be: I must have enjoyed it, because I didn't say anything, so it must have satisfied me. But now, it's a variety of feelings. Counselling touched the tip of the iceberg. It's still day-to-day trying to work it out. Counselling tells you it wasn't your fault. But it doesn't really address those heavy feelings inside.

> I liked it, so I must have done something to encourage it. Maybe not in the beginning, but afterwards. On one level, I know it's not my fault. I fully understand that no matter what I did to encourage it, I was still a child. If my daughter does something wrong, it's up to me to tell her so. Likewise, it was his responsibility to take care of me and to help me stop; and not to participate with me in helping me to be harmful. Part of taking care of me was to stop me being naughty – even if I pulled down his zipper and stuck it in me, it was still his fault.

> It was pleasurable. It makes me feel guilty to say I liked

> him to touch my breasts . . . My brother also used to play with my breasts. I used to play sexual games with my little brother. It fills me with horror to talk about it even now.

The guilt, horror and revulsion that many of us who have been sexually abused feel when we begin to face the abuse is acute. How can it be, we ask ourselves, that, at times, we desired our fathers and felt pleasure from the sex and the closeness and the cuddles that the sitting on laps gave us?

Everyone wants the closeness and the feeling of being wanted or special. It is not wrong to experience such feelings. Usually it is these feelings which incest survivors most often remember, says Sonia Francis. But, along with it is often a feeling of ambivalence towards the abuser. As well as the memory of the closeness and of being special, there is the anger and frustration, as well as an awareness, however vague, that the sexual aspect of the relationship was wrong.

Sonia Francis notes that:

> Sometimes an incest survivor will come to me, and it can be a bit like the flavour of the month. They come with a specific agenda, e.g., – I want sympathy. But they tend not to acknowledge their part within the abuse. It is important to shift their understanding to sort out the feelings – particularly when brothers are involved in the incest, and there is much more of an equal participation in it; and then they later find out that what they did was called incest.[5]

Francis believes that 'it's not about fault or blame. It's about what you generally feel yourself. It can be confusing if you think you should feel angry and you really enjoyed it. You begin to think: "I must really be a terrible person."'

In her work with black women survivors of incest, Francis notes that in some cases the starting point is to decide about the abuse: 'We begin with the question of whether it was abuse at the time or whether it is abuse now that they've read that that's what it was.'

She makes the important proviso that this criterion is only used in some cases, where the child was old enough to experience a feeling of moral right and wrong. If, for example the incest involves a two-year-old, there is no room for ambivalence about what is clearly a case of serious abuse. In very early abuse, notes Francis, the abuse is very often buried deep within the subconscious, and tends to come out through dreams, even though on a conscious level the victim does not remember it. One woman had a recurring dream of being on a slab, with a presence of striped pyjamas pressing down on her. When the dream was unpacked, she came to realise that she had been abused before the age of three.

But what about those of us who were aware of the abuse from the beginning, and who were old enough to realise, from the beginning, that what was happening was not really supposed to happen? How do we cope with the guilt that keeps gnawing away at our psyches, returning to haunt us when we least expect it or maybe can least handle it?

As noted earlier, the Wyatt study pointed to the tendency of Afro-American women to look internally for reasons for their abuse. Wyatt adds:

> This finding, along with Afro-American women's highly negative reaction to abuse, their tendency not to disclose incidents as often to nuclear family members or to police and to disclose abuse to extended family members, some of whom have been found to abuse them, place Afro-American women at risk for more severe consequences of abuse.[6]

The consequence for many of us is an emotional juggling act which involves balancing the guilt that we carry with us

– when we face it – against the knowledge that, by keeping silent, we colluded, participated and enjoyed it, even. We grasp the guilt unto us – assuming the burden of blame, though it threatens to engulf us.

Therapist Pat Agana often counsels women who begin therapy with the statement, 'I know I was guilty, because if I hadn't liked it, I wouldn't have done it.' Her answer to that, far from being a sop just to make the women feel better is to say, 'He was the adult. You didn't scream, but if you had done you might have been killed or hurt in some way. Being a child, you made the decision that you felt best.' Simple words, but oh so hard to really take on board if you can remember, but at the same time, oh so important if you do.

Coming to terms with the guilt, says Agana, 'is the last great hurdle for many women who have been abused'.[7] It is, she notes, about learning to love yourself, because until we *can* love ourselves, our capacity to love others is limited.

Resolving the guilt

The ways in which we go about coping with our guilty feelings and memories about those sexual episodes from our childhoods are as individual as we are. For a long time I could not reconcile the guilty feelings I very much carried around with me. I used to work at ignoring those memories (I could sometimes do it for long periods). I also became an achiever. At one point I tried to resolve them by closing off from men and any suggestion of a relationship with one. I was like this from the time of the incest through to early adulthood.

It was hard for me to make the leap from regarding those things my dad did with me (which, by now I was certain were wrong) as OK to do with someone who wasn't my father. It was all so confusing. When I began to make steps towards accepting an attraction to men, they were hesitant and unsure. It is very hard to let go of the guilt and self-blame. I am not sure I have let go of it entirely.

It is less confusing now, because my rational, adult self can explore it in depth. It has to do with needing closeness and intimacy, and being afraid of what you'll find in its place. It has to do with being able to trust and to be rewarded with trust in return. It has to do with continuing to seek love, and finding it in the most unlikely places.

For me, a big part of guilt resolution is being believed: without condemnation, without judgement, without censure. It has gone a long way towards giving me the space I need to explore all those painful and confusing memories.

Thoughts on love

I believe that for some of us our active participation in our own abuse was a way of saying, 'Love me'. To understand this in its non-judgemental entirety, it is necessary to separate the purely pleasurable aspect represented by biological sex from the emotional loving which is as much a life-enhancing necessity for most women as is eating. It is on this level, this emotional plane, that such participation should be examined. It concerns the attempts by many of us who have been abused to transcend the baseness of the sex act itself, and to focus on the warm envelopment which occurred as a result of being close, intimate and loved by someone.

Hugs and kisses. Love. Much love. Simple enough concepts. Jotted down at the end of a note or letter to a close friend, they impart the required degree of salutary greeting and affection. Yet how many of us actually experience the love which is so easily implied by such postscripts? For many of us, love, or the outward display of it, is restricted to almost mechanical displays or expressions of affection – the peck on the cheek; the blown kiss; the casual hug. If we were asked to say what love is to us, each of us, I would bet, could come up with a more full-bodied expression of what it means to us.

For black women, however, locked as we are in an ethos which ascribes hardness, harshness and an unlovable nature to us, this does not come easily. Historically, in order to survive, black women have had to grow thick skins. Shedding those skins, and leaving ourselves open to the vulnerability that can flow from saying, 'I love you, or I want to be loved by you', is a prospect fraught with risk. But one which is desired no less.

Though I didn't know it on a conscious level when I was twelve and accepting of the 'loving' that my father gave me, looking back on it now I feel that what I wanted, needed, and should have had instead, was the kind of love which took note of those all-important boundaries between a father and a daughter. I wanted my father to be my friend as well as a loving father. I wanted, needed protection and care from my father. What I got was sex.

I don't know if my father felt he was caring for me and protecting me in his own way. I don't think I'll ever know, even if he were alive to tell me. I'm not even sure he knew. It may simply have been that he transferred my mother's rejection of him to the nearest and most available person like her, in an effort to achieve the kind of love for which *he* was looking. I don't know if it was purely biological for him, or if he truly did love me and showed it how he felt best. What I do know is that those moments of snatched and furtive sexual activity we engaged in have left me reeling from the impact for the past thirty years, and still trying to sort out my own innocence or guilt about choosing to love my father or allowing him to love me in that way.

My story is not unusual. There are so many black women

needing love; love which – in the way that we desire it: genuine, real and committed – is not easy to find. Often we have to be content with second best; to make the best of the situations which frame our lives – sometimes that is good, sometimes bad or indifferent. In the end we need to move on. For black women who were sexually abused as children, and who can remember that they looked for love within their abuse, there is no moving on, however, until we can face the demons from those memories squarely and truthfully. One survivor said:

> The spin-off from all of this is that I have other memories which are clear – of being nine years old and seeing other people doing it [making love]. I got into the habit of thinking that this was how to get comfort . . . I needed the attention of some male figures. Several times after, I got myself into situations where people were still putting their hands up my knickers.

We should also bear in mind the following:

> The sexual aspect of these relationships has nothing in common with romantic or seductive dreams. The words fondle or caress, researchers say, are better replaced by grab, rub, probe, lick and suck. But because of its hidden nature ('our little secret,' an abusing father may say), sexual abuse can become an activity that the child may want and even derive pleasure from. Only later may the experience feel abusive. The abuser may therefore argue that the child agreed to sex or even led him on. But in the context of a relationship between a child and a trusted adult who is used to being obeyed, acquiescence can never be equated with consent.
>
> A few studies have suggested that some children may survive this kind of sexual contact with an adult unscathed. But most researchers are sceptical. The abused show 'more frequent signs of maladjustment and general unhappiness than the non abused' . . . They suffer a 'significant distortion'

> of their emotional lives, of the 'future pattern of their sexual activities,' and of their ability to parent.[8]

We blame ourselves. We carry the guilt. We feel we are dirty, worthless, and unworthy of love. We feel we are horrible people for allowing such a thing to happen to us, when we knew, deep down, that it was wrong. And it is the moving away from these feelings – which after all are the consequences of our accepting love, as we found it – that must be our task in recovering and feeling good about ourselves again.

(In the end, I have found the kind of love which I needed for my soul and for my salvation. I came close, once, to finding it with a black man. It is a white man, however, who has been my partner for the past 20 years.)

Just say no – women, children and refusing/telling: the reality behind the slogan

> Now, when I was growing up, there was no 'Just Say No' programs, no television coverage, no Oprah Winfrey show – there was no one to talk to about this mountain that I faced. I wondered what I had done to invite this invasion of my person, this assault against what I had been taught was good and decent behavior?[9]

Before we can begin the important task of recovery it's necessary to examine some of the baggage which gets in the way of our establishing and maintaining a positive self-regard. One of the main stumbling blocks is the idea that if we had just said no to our abuser, it wouldn't have happened. This argument is often used against women who have been sexually abused; in particular, rape victims, who are expected to thwart their attackers by the simple act of saying no.

A study carried out by the Child Abuse Studies Unit at the

Polytechnic of North London makes important comments regarding the concept of just saying no as a method of preventing child sexual abuse. The 1991 study examined the prevalence of sexual abuse in a sample of 1,200 16–21-years-olds who were attending further education colleges in England, Scotland and Wales.

The study found that

> one-fifth of the experiences reported were attempts – in which the actions of the child/young person resulted in them escaping or avoiding the assault. Some of these were attempted rapes and abductions. The strategies used included 'saying no', physically resisting, running away and avoiding the abuser. However *these same strategies were also used by 90 per cent of those who were unable to stop the abuse.*[10] (Emphasis added)

The report also said:

> About half of those who had experienced abuse told someone about the abuse at the time. The person they told was most likely to be a female friend or relative. Fewer than one in ten was disbelieved, but the major reason given for not telling anyone was fear of being disbelieved. Only five per cent of incidents were ever reported to any agency; and of 1,051 incidents only 10 resulted in any form of prosecution.

The researchers noted that, 'the fact that so many children and young people actively resist sexual abuse suggests that safety programmes with simple "no, go tell" messages may be teaching our grandchildren to suck eggs. They are not "prevention" since they are effective in one out of five cases. Prevention requires finding ways to stop abusers abusing.'

It is clear from these findings that just saying no is not going to stop child sexual abuse. An examination of the responses of black women survivors' experience also bears this out.

> When I was 12, I was babysitting for an aunt. She was in hospital to have another baby. Her husband came home at four in the morning. I woke up with his thing between my legs. I said: 'No! And if you make me turn round I will scream.' It didn't stop him. He had an orgasm, but he didn't penetrate me. He just came between my thighs.

'The more we teach our children to say no, the more abusers will find other ways,' said one survivor. 'I don't fear the stigma of disclosure. I fear that it [abuse] will go underground even more in such a way that we can't detect it.'

Another aspect to do with just saying no is that children do hold the guilt and pain inside, and carry it with them to adulthood – if they make it to adulthood, that is. What are the consequences to a child's psyche if they don't say no? 'When I work with abused children now,' said one black social worker/survivor, 'they say to me: "But I took the smarties!" And if you say to a child that it wasn't their fault, they think you don't understand. You actually have to work it through with them and get beyond it.'

Getting beyond the incest is not so easy for many survivors. You only have to read the newspaper headlines to see why just saying no is not an easy or viable option for many children who have been incestuously abused. The catalogue of violent retribution for girls and women who have said no or disclosed about their abuse, even in these so-called enlightened times of facing up to child sexual abuse more honestly and vigorously, is sobering.

The shocking case of a fourteen-year-old girl in London who 'suffered a slow and agonising death by electrocution at the hands of her stepfather after she accused him of sexually abusing her' (*Guardian*, 19 February 1992) is one instance where a child said no and tragically suffered the consequences.

Nor is the problem of saying no confined to children. The recently acknowledged phenomenon of date rape is one example where saying no does not always work, even for adults and especially for women, as the following story (reported in the *Guardian*, 14 May 1991) of a Syracuse University student, who was raped by a former boyfriend, shows:

> I'd had a real teenage crush on this guy for months. Finally, he asked me out and we slept together once. But I knew he wanted to sleep with other people, too, and I didn't want that kind of relationship, so I broke it off.
>
> One night I called him, just to talk, and a couple of nights later he arrived at my house, drunk. One of my housemates let him in and he just walked into my room and climbed into bed with me. I was still half asleep. He said, 'I know what you were asking for, the other night on the phone.' I kept saying no, but I didn't scream. I was embarrassed; I didn't want my housemates to hear.

One incest survivor put it this way: 'I'm 23. It's taken me 12 years to say no.' In Britain, further ambiguities have been raised as a result of the Cleveland child abuse enquiry. In particular, allegations of child sexual abuse have been called into question because of the methods used in diagnosing the abuse. These ambiguities must lead us to ask ourselves whether a child's ability to say no or disclose the occurrence of sexual abuse is compromised or rendered ineffective, when balanced against the more dominant ethic of parental rights; and whether, as a result, a child's saying no simply cannot prevent the abuse, or, once it has occurred, ensure punishment of the perpetrator.

A recent case, with allegations of ritual abuse involving two sisters just outside London, was thrown out of court because the prosecuting attorney told the judge, 'he could no longer rely on the evidence of a 10-year-old girl, who had spent four days in the witness box. She had claimed that she and her sister were subjected to sex assaults during satanic rituals in Epping Forest, in Essex.' According to the [male] judge, the girl's evidence was 'so uncertain, inconsistent and improbable' that it would not be right to seek a conviction; and that the prosecution decision to drop the case was 'entirely proper' (*Guardian*, 20 November 1991).

With indicators such as these, the obvious conclusion is that saying no and telling frequently doesn't get survivors of child sexual abuse the protection they need nor the redress they seek.

> Central to judicial thinking and practice relating to sexual offences has been the assumption that women and children are liars . . . This idea is still embodied in the law which makes it obligatory for a judge to warn a jury that it is 'dangerous to convict' for a sexual offence solely on the evidence of an alleged victim. Without corroboration such as medical evidence, or a witness to the assault, the evidence of women and children is seen as inherently unreliable. This corroboration rule applies in no other situation, except cases in which a prosecution witness has been an accomplice to the crime. The implications are clear – women and children alleging sexual assaults are given the legal status of accomplices.[11]

The Children Act

In Britain, the recently instituted Children Act enshrines in statutory law the ambiguities regarding children and their rights in resisting sexual abuse. Though its main purpose is to protect the rights of children, it aims to balance this with parental powers of responsibility for children. The result is a law on the statute books which enshrines parental dominance in deference to the furore caused by the perceived erosion of parental rights in the wake of the Cleveland child abuse enquiry and other notorious child abuse cases. It remains to be seen how well the act accomplishes its balancing act. But it is important to remember that: (1) children must be first and foremost *listened* to about *any* allegations of such abuse; and (2) action should be taken if and where necessary, based on what they have to say.

Black women and children and saying no

But where do black children (and women) who say no fit into all of this? The recent case in Indianapolis of Desirée Washington, the Miss Black America beauty contestant who successfully prosecuted boxer Mike Tyson for rape, provides an important object lesson, within the context of black communities, on the penalties and consequences for black women and children who say no. Washington reported that in the lead-up to the trial she was approached by members of the black community, including black churchmen, who advocated Tyson's role as a victim. Why would such upstanding citizens take it upon themselves to save Tyson's skin at the expense of the *real* victim in all of this?

In an article entitled, 'Harlem directs anger at accuser' (*Guardian*, 12 February 1992), it was reported that popular sentiment in the heart of Harlem was 'overwhelmingly in favour of Mike Tyson and against the woman who accused him of rape . . . the feeling was widespread among shopkeepers [e.g.] that Tyson had got a bum rap. If the case had been in New York, said one youngster, Tyson "would have got off".'

The Reverend T.J. Jemison, head of the 7.5-million-strong National Baptist Convention, and one of a number of black leaders to petition the court for clemency for Tyson, argued that Tyson symbolised 'the black male and his plight' (*Guardian*, 27 March 1992).

The situation was decidedly not one of, Sister Washington, we understand and sympathise with *your* plight; but, Sister! How could you do this to a black man and the black community? I ask again: Who *is* the community?

Likewise, the denigration of Professor Anita Hill, whose allegations of sexual harassment against Judge Clarence Thomas provide another case in point. The outcry which resulted from some members of America's black community, who perceived Hill's testimony as an assault on black manhood, was painful to watch. Such was the vehemence of those denouncing her that a group of African-American women (African American Women in Defense of Ourselves) were moved to take out a full-page ad in the *New York Times*, reprinted in *Essence* (March 1992) in support of Hill. It read in part:

> We are particularly outraged by the racist and sexist treatment of Professor Anita Hill, an African-American woman who was maligned and castigated for daring to speak publicly of her own experience of sexual abuse. The malicious defamation of Professor Hill insulted all women of African descent and sent a dangerous message to any woman who might contemplate a sexual-harassment complaint.
>
> We speak here because we recognise that the media are now portraying the Black community as prepared to tolerate both the dismantling of affirmative action and the evil of sexual harassment in order to have any Black man on the Supreme Court. We want to make clear that the media have ignored or distorted many African-American voices. We will not be silenced . . . this country, which has a long legacy of racism and sexism, has never taken the sexual abuse of Black women seriously. Throughout U.S. history Black women have been sexually stereotyped as immoral, insatiable, perverse, the initiators in all sexual contacts – abusive or otherwise. The common assumption in legal proceedings as well as in the larger society has been that Black women cannot be raped or otherwise sexually abused. As Anita Hill's experience demonstrates, Black women who speak of these matters are not likely to be believed.

Anita Hill has said of her ordeal, and in response to those who level the accusation that she betrayed a black man,

> It was a tough decision, but I have to live with my conscience as a Black woman. It doesn't do any good as Black people to hide what we believe is wrong because it may be perceived as a betrayal. It's an unfortunate and awful position for Black women to be in. It's interesting that people haven't seen the harassment of Black women as a betrayal.[12]

What chance do little black girls have of saying no in the face of such concerted hectoring, by some in our black communities, towards girls and women who *do* say no? It is not difficult to understand that their options are limited if they try to buck such an inherently and doubly abusive system. But sexism is not the only thing that militates against just saying no. An examination of the nature of the (disciplinarian) relationship between adults and children in black communities is also important. In the words of one survivor:

> It has a lot to do with our belief systems. For example, 'what happens in the home, stays in the home.' 'You respect your elders and you're never rude to them.' It affects children who should be encouraged to get help. But black families don't work in that way. There was no way I could go to anybody for help. We should look at the way parents work with children and perhaps they should try to address this. Plus, there are the ideas we instill in our children: Like with friends of the family. We are told to respect what they do, no matter what. They don't always do good things, they do bad ones as well. It's about children having views and rights. It's about accepting that children do have opinions.

Another incest survivor thought that 'just saying no' was only a first step. 'It's not the end. You say No, because I don't like it, and No, you shouldn't do this – but children who are seven or eight may not be able to make that clear. The first step is to realise that it's wrong – but it takes time and courage.'

A black woman survivor who works with children who have been sexually abused put it this way:

> We come up with ideas for them to say. Just to say no is nothing, because a child is already emotionally upset and powerless anyway. I'm not there if it happens. They can't come to me if they have to do this [be sexually abused]. We tell them to tell the police, or someone else in authority – to find a suitable adult. But it's difficult to get across to a child that 'This adult is OK, but that adult isn't.'
>
> Children can understand it if you say that it was wrong for this man to offer you sweets. But they also know that adults are supposed to care for them, and are not supposed to harm you. Children should be empowered, but they can't handle all this – saying no requires too much power.

In short, many black women who have been abused feel that teaching black children to say no is fine as far as it goes. But, as can be seen, it does not go very far. It is only one approach, and a not very effective one for most black children, or indeed for many people who have been sexually abused.

CHAPTER 5

Towards a black feminist understanding of child sexual abuse

I write this as a black woman committed to equality of opportunity for all women – as a feminist. I write especially for black women, whose image as 'long-suffering victims [has kept those of us who have survived it] passive and confused about the abuse in our lives'. I recognise that as a concept, feminism among black women has been slow to gain ground. The struggle of black feminists has been and continues to be waged on an upward slope as we try to move feminism beyond the toe-hold position it occupies within our communities. Yet for black feminists the dream/commitment to spreading the gospel of feminism, one which embraces the concept of equality of opportunity regardless of gender, race, class or sexual preference, remains a strong one.

I define black feminism as maintaining a physical, mental, spiritual and emotional well-being, as well as economic, political and social opportunities on an equal basis with men. For me, to be black and feminist means that I take that well-worn, but true phrase, 'the personal is the political' very much to heart. It conditions my beliefs as a woman, as a black person and as a survivor of incest. In a wider sense, a feminist understanding must also encompass other forms of sexual abuse against black girls and black women. For I believe that a feminist view crucially informs an understanding of the male abuse of power against women and children. I believe that once we realise how the system of patriarchy works, then such an understanding can facilitate, for those of us who have been sexually abused, a realisation of how and why it happened to us. We can begin to see, in fact, that it is a logical extension of the male preserve, as it is currently defined.

> The social response to the physical 'damage' of the rape victim makes extremely difficult the reconciliation of the feelings related with the loss of virginity in the woman. Objectively, if a woman is a virgin and is raped, after the sexual assault she will continue to be a woman and a virgin. Nevertheless, it is a pity that socially, virginity is more valuable in its physical component than in its spiritual and moral qualities. Vaginal lacerations or a scar in the hymen in no way can change a woman's reputation, integrity, purity or honesty. *The only thing that could change in a woman after a forcible rape is her consciousness.*[1] (Emphasis added)

Incest and child sexual abuse – why does it happen? Observations from a feminist perspective

> We believe that what feminism offers us is not a 'blueprint' but a perspective for looking at the world . . . It is a perspective that acknowledges the unequal distribution of power between women and men in society, a set of relations which is institutionalised within the family, and that sees child sexual abuse as an abuse of male power, and a betrayal of trust.[2]

The sexual oppression which exists in black communities makes the development of a black feminist perspective on incest and child sexual abuse long overdue. This oppression allows the tacit acceptance of incest and CSA in our communities. The situation is one in which the abuse (whether incest, rape or domestic violence) is almost regarded as a man's *by right* if sexual gratification is not forthcoming from more appropriate avenues. The justification seems to be that it is deemed appropriate that men achieve sexual fulfilment by the nearest available means.

The need to address the sexism in our communities is a necessary part of the development of a black feminist analysis about incest and CSA – but it is not the only thing that is necessary. Such an analysis must also be concerned with attacking racist stereotypes about black women's and men's sexuality. A conference held in London several years ago brought together black and white feminists in an exercise to frame a feminist response to child sexual abuse. It contained the following statement about the need to develop an anti-racist as well as anti-sexist framework:

> A feminist practice is not inherently an anti-racist one. This conference has on its agenda developing an anti-racist practice on child sexual abuse. If the myths on child sexual abuse have been damaging, some of the most damaging have related child sexual abuse to race; if intervention has been traumatising, some of the worst has been white intervention in black lives. Especially damaging to people abused can be the internalisation of badness as blackness that racism can produce. So anti-racism is on the Agenda.[3]

The black feminist perspective must address the need to deal with the sexual oppression that victimises us in our communities; and also the racism which has been apparent both in wider society and within the women's movement, in the sensitive area of black people and sexuality.

It has taken a long time for black feminists to begin discussions which focus on our sexuality. In the late 1970s and early 1980s in Britain we began halting discussions, after much prodding by some amongst us. We undertook these discourses with trepidation and fears that even talking about our sexuality could lay us open to allegations of navel contemplation, demonstrating a lack of political seriousness, or would be misconstrued, resulting in the label of 'lesbian' being attached to us by anti-feminists and others in our communities. This was a very hot potato, indeed. The homophobia which exists in black communities posed a real stumbling block to addressing issues about our sexuality. As black feminists having to fight on many fronts and for every inch of acceptance in our communities, we were acutely aware of the minefield such discussions represented.

Had we begun those discussions with less trepidation and more determination to sort out our own ambiguities as far as sex and sexuality were concerned, I think (with hindsight) that we would have ridden the storm (which they precipitated) in a stronger position, and maybe preserved more of our collective psyches with far less pain and doubt. We might even have been able to help some sisters, like me, to open up sooner about their sexual abuse, and move forward in sisterly fashion, with a view to getting rid of some of the pain, guilt and confusion. Maybe we would not now be in the position of playing 'catch-up' in dealing with this crucial area.

That said, I recognise the limitations imposed on us as black women. Though in an ideal world we should have been able to cope and to help each other cope successfully with these aspects, in reality we were all stymied by circumstances and conditioning which worked against as full an undertaking of issues of sex and sexuality as was needed.

The Brixton Black Women's Group (BWG) was my feminist home for the 1970s and 1980s until its demise in the late 1980s. It was there that I learned my feminism as a black woman. It was there that I forged the relationships and the friendships that have seen me through many years of campaigning, discussion and activism. But equally clear to me was that for all my years of involvement with BWG, it was there, too, that I found little space, had I wished it, within which to confront my contradictions and confusion about my sexuality, particularly as it related to me as a survivor of incest. Why?

To try to understand the difficulty that even progressive black women had and (still, to some extent) have in raising the issues of sex and sexuality for group discussion, it must be viewed within the context of the implications of such talk in our communities, generally; and in particular, the reticence which punctuates this sphere of relations between black men and black women. By and large, our communities are closed to such discussions. We are uncomfortable with sexuality out in the open (a fact which makes the media stereotypes of black people as sexual animals all the more ironic).

When I was young, my developing sexuality was, I knew, not a topic which could be discussed – I didn't even know how to speak to my grandmother about such things. Her main concern anyway was that first and foremost should come self-sufficiency and resilience for a black woman. I was taught that I had to be able to make my own way in the world. My experience was very different from that of the white girls who were my contemporaries and who were conditioned to regard success in terms of acquiring wifely virtues and motherhood. (It was these same white girls, who, as women, in the late 1960s and 1970s threw off this oppressive yoke and formed the feminist movement.) I was not, in the main, brought up to regard marriage as my first option. I knew that I had to get an education, and a job or career – as a teacher maybe or a nurse – and then think about men. I can still hear my grandmother saying: 'The Lord knows, life was hard enough out there for black people and black women, without making things worse for yourself by staying poor with no education. You're going to need that education, girl.'

Writer Michele Wallace described this process of socialisation for black, female children in *Black Macho & The Myth of the Superwoman*:

> I can't remember when I first learned that my family expected me to work, to be able to take care of myself when I grew up. My mother was so extraordinarily career-oriented that I was never allowed to take lessons in anything unless I manifested a deep interest in a career in that area . . . It had been drilled into me that the best and only sure support was self-support.
>
> The fact that my family expected me to work and have a career should have made the things I wanted very different from what little white girls wanted according to the popular sociological view. But I don't believe any sociologist took into account a man like my stepfather. My stepfather gave me 'housewife lessons.' It was he who taught me how to clean house and how I should act around men. 'Don't be like your mother,' he told me. 'She's a nice lady but she's a bad wife. She was just lucky with me. I want you to get a *good* husband.'[4]

Wallace's account also neatly sums up the predicament of black girls as regards their sexuality. On the one hand, we were taught by our mothers or grandmothers or aunts to challenge the gender-specific roles laid down for women, to be self-sufficient, without having to rely on a man. On the other hand, challenging gender stereotypes about our sexuality was rarely touched upon in any kind of meaningful or useful way. Wallace relates that the women in her life (mother, aunts) had 'nearly all been divorced at least once', and that 'men always seemed peripheral to their lives'. That strikes a chord from my own childhood. But the discordant note comes from the fact that although men were viewed as on the periphery the unspoken epithet which accompanied such attitudes was that, nevertheless, it was better to have one around than not. Though we knew that black women could do it all if they chose to, it was more respectable somehow, more reassuring, to have a man somewhere in the background.

Perhaps because of this view of black men on the periphery there was not the need for a rigorous examination of any frailties that may have been a part of the black male psyche. Included in this must be ideas which address their sexual proclivities and entitlements, as balanced against those of the black female.

My grandmother did tell me to keep my dress down and my legs closed. I can remember thinking that it was already too late for that advice. The message I got was that it was my responsibility to control the male sexual urge by modifying my own behaviour; instead of directly challenging the underlying assumptions which gave men an unspoken assurance to accost me in the first place.

Those lessons about self-sufficiency which I learned were good ones. But it probably never occurred to my grandmother to add that though I had a right to say no to male sexual advances because of the goal to be self-sufficient, I also had the right because being male does not in and of itself bestow an inalienable entitlement to sexual gratification, whatever the cost; whatever the consequences.

My counsel to my own children will be aimed at making this distinction clearer. For my daughter, I will pass on the legacy of her right to say no because her body is her own, to do with as she chooses. That, ultimately, the choice should be hers, unblinkered by questionable considerations of ideas about male sexuality and what that may or may not entail. For my son, I wish to engender the idea that he has no automatic right, over and above that of any woman, to be sexually gratified because he happens to be male. As Audre Lorde said in her essay on raising a male child:

> I wish to raise a Black man who will recognize that the legitimate objects of his hostility are not women, but the particulars of a structure that programs him to fear and despise women as well as his own Black self.[5]

The failure of our communities, and in particular many black women, to embrace feminist principles has meant that the inequities associated with sexuality continue to place black girls and black women at a disadvantage. The process of undoing the damage caused by the sexual abuse of children is an arduous one. The problem is that of the male dynamic of power over females; but it also has to do with the inability or the unwillingness, by some, though not all, to examine the conscious or unconscious sanction for uncontrolled male sexual gratification.

A speech by counsellor and women's health activist Pat Agana eloquently frames what this failure to grasp the nettle of gender relations in black communities can mean in the context of child sexual abuse:

> In October 1989 I attended the Caribbean Regional Conference on Child Abuse and Neglect. That was an eye opener . . . In that conference some thirty Africans who had been sexually abused as children came together to discuss their experience. All the evidence I needed that it is an issue which concerns us here in Britain.
>
> Child sexual abuse is not a new phenomenon. Each and every one of us can relay stories from our childhood about particular individuals in our communities who were said to be strange or it was said that they were the father of their daughter's child. These tales may have been whispered but we all know of them.[6]

Gender and roles

> There is a woman. She lives in a world, this world, in which power is real. Men have it, generally speaking; she does not because she is a woman. She is devalued not only in people's thoughts but in the way she is treated: by individuals because she is not their equal; by institutions of the society – law, religion, art, education . . . The ways in which she is devalued are concrete, material, real: sexual, economic, physical, social. They happen to her: not as a disembodied spirit but as a corporeal being, flesh and blood. Inferiority is done to her: it is real and she is real.[7]

Racism and sexism combine to militate against what should be black women's unassailable right to self-determination and freedom from oppression. Historically, we have been constricted on the one hand by our absolute need to work for the survival of ourselves and our communities in the face of unrelenting racism and hostility. On the other, we are chastised for daring to survive, indeed for the quality of our survival. Angela Davis wrote about our predicament in this way:

> Like their men, Black women have worked until they could work no more. Like their men, they have assumed the responsibilities of family providers. The unorthodox feminine qualities of assertiveness and self-reliance – for which Black women have been frequently praised but more often rebuked – are reflections of their labor and their struggles outside the home. But like their white sisters called 'housewives,' they have cooked and cleaned and have nurtured and reared untold numbers of children. But unlike the white housewives, who learned to lean on their husbands for economic security, Black wives and mothers, usually workers as well, have rarely been offered the time and energy to become experts at domesticity. Like their white working-class sisters, who also carry the double burden of

> working for a living and servicing husbands and children, Black women have needed relief from this oppressive predicament for a long, long time.[8]

Again, myths play their part in threatening black women's survival. Myths about our roles and the alleged damage this does to black males, especially. Michele Wallace succinctly outlines the essence of the myth/roles of black women in the following passage:

> Sapphire. Mammy. Tragic mulatto wench. Workhorse, can swing an axe, lift a load, pick cotton with any man. A wonderful housekeeper. Excellent with children. Very clean. Very religious. A terrific mother. A great little singer and dancer and a devoted teacher and social worker. She's always had more opportunities than the black man because she was no threat to the white man so he made it easy for her. But curiously enough, she frequently ends up on welfare. Nevertheless, she is more educated and makes more money than the black man. She is more likely to be employed and more likely to be a professional than the black man. And subsequently she provides the main support for the family. Not beautiful, rather hard looking unless she has white blood, but then very beautiful. The black ones are exotic though, great in bed, tigers. And very fertile. If she is middle class she tends to be uptight about sex, prudish. She is hard on and unsupportive of black men, domineering, castrating. She tends to wear the pants around her house. Very strong. Sorrow rolls right off her brow like so much rain. Tough, unfeminine. Opposed to women's rights movements, considers herself already liberated. Nevertheless, unworldly. Definitely not a dreamer, rigid, inflexible, uncompassionate, lacking in goals any more imaginative than a basket of fried chicken and a good fuck.[9]

Equally, however, black men are also constrained – by another set of stereotypes. A similar mythological role depiction of the black male would probably read as follows:

> Stud. Over-sexed animal. Strong young Buck. Hard worker.

> Uppity at times but can be whipped back into shape. Not to be trusted around white women. Craves white women, especially if he is middle class. Brutal to black women. Dominated by black women. Downtrodden because of domineering black women. Unemployed and unemployable. Low self-esteem. High mortality rate. Strung out on dope. As likely to die from being shot as from drug overdose. Good looking. Fancies himself a ladies' man. Mr Preacher Man. Mr Pimp. Mr Drug Pusher. Mr Lawyer, Doctor, Businessman. Can take him out of the ghetto, but can't take the ghetto out of him. Fathers children and leaves them. Weak but proud. Violent. Ill-educated. Bit slow on the uptake. Braggadocio. Liar.

These stereotypical strait-jackets, which we, as black people, are also guilty of believing we fit into at times, are responsible, in large part, for the problems which have prevented an honest, frank and empathetic exploration of relations between black women and black men. We are all victimised because of these mythical attributes being assigned to us and believed by ourselves and others. Thankfully, there are signs now, especially in the United States, that black women and black men are beginning to tackle this huge gulf which has grown up between us.

Referring to Toni Morrison's example of good relationships between black women and black men explored in her book *Beloved,* writer bell hooks has noted,

> Morrison evokes a notion of bonding that may be rooted in passion, desire, even romantic love, but the point of connection between black women and men is that space of recognition and understanding, where we know one another so well, our histories, that we can take the bits and pieces, the fragments of who we are, and put them back together, re-member them. It is this joy of intellectual bonding, of working together to create liberatory theory and analysis that black women and men can give one another.[10]

It is not too late; it can never be too late, for we both need each other. But there is still a long way to go. It is painful, as well as alarming, for example, to hear a black man say in 1992 that there just aren't many good black women out there. But that is exactly what a black male friend said to me not long ago. He felt that too many black women were too hostile to black men, in general. All a black woman wants to do, he said, is make the black man look bad, and not give him support. He felt that most black women only want to make it for themselves in the white man's world.

It is equally painful to know that the mirror views among some black women I talk to is that black men are uncaring, untrustworthy, unable to demonstrate real affection, and lacking in emotional maturity. I hasten to add that this is *not* intended as a universal statement on the relations between black men and black women. It is a subject which requires a book (or several) on its own.

But we need to be aware that attitudes such as these, which are held by some black people, create the kind of climate where it was possible for Desirée Washington to be victimised and disbelieved by the *black* communities in Indianapolis and New York for bringing rape charges against Mike Tyson. Such attitudes also help to explain (though not excuse) why Anita Hill had to respond to accusations of betraying the black community. I believe that such attitudes also account for why the sexual abuse of black girls and women is rarely acknowledged or even more rarely discussed and regarded as a problem in black communities.

Sexual harassment, violence and exploitation of women transcends class and race boundaries. Black and white men, regardless of their class position, align with each other on the basis of shared sexism. The consequences of this for black communities are that black men who are victimised by racism in common with black women also collude, as males, to oppress black women in a sexist way.

This belies a failure to understand the dynamics of class structures which seek to undermine the cohesion of black communities. Some black men (and it is my argument that it is mainly these men who sexually abuse black girls and women) fail to make the connection between racism and sexism. They play out their sexist and sexualised aggression with black girls/women as the losers. Black men who commit sexual abuse against children devalue us as a community of people and undermine attempts to throw off stereotypes and work towards shared and equitable solutions for all.

The sexism of some black men and the racism of white society results in a reluctance by some black women survivors of incest and CSA to name their abusers and therein take control of their lives. If a woman does take action, and goes to the police for example, she is likely to be condemned by her own community for betrayal and to have her own sexuality called into question by the wider community, thus reinforcing the stereotypes. If she doesn't, she is left with maintaining the silence which gives tacit approval to the abuse, and thus undervalues her own worth as a participating and *equal* member of the community.

I view the task of black feminists as being to work towards overcoming this compulsion to blame black women for their own abuse. It is a struggle which must make us question any knee-jerk tendency to treat women as mindless objects or body parts. As black women, we should be arguing for a respect which recognises the mutual right of black women and black men to break free of the confines laid down by others; confines which have conspired to keep us all victims, by dividing one from the other. My argument is for the right to live our lives unfettered, and on our own terms; with the roles we occupy being roles that are defined by ourselves.

Expectations

In her novel *Meridian* Alice Walker focuses on the Civil Rights Movement in the United States during the 1960s. Among other things, she examines the frailties of some black men, who failed to understand the black woman, or her reasons for being in the front line of the struggle. In particular, Walker concentrates on the narrow frame of reference mapped out for the black woman by the black man.

Meridian is a high school drop-out in the deep South. She is also an abandoned mother. She makes the decision to leave her child in the capable hands of its paternal grandmother; travels outside the South; acquires an education and becomes a part of the Civil Rights Movement. She meets Truman, a black man who is also part of the Movement, and gives her love to him. Eventually, however, she becomes disillusioned by the hypocrisy she finds – in both the personal and political sense – within the Movement.

To save her sanity as well as her life, she journeys back to the people who make up the strong weathered roots of her heritage. There she finds sustenance and survival. She makes her journey alone, without Truman. It is a decision he finds impossible to understand. In the following extract, Meridian and Truman speak of the way in which her love for him has changed in the process of her spiritual rebirth:

> 'Hah,' he said bitterly, 'why don't you admit you learned to hate me; to disrespect me, to wish I was dead. It was your contempt for me that made it impossible for me to forget.'
>
> Meridian: 'I meant it when I said it [her love] sets you free. You are free to be whichever way you like, to be with whoever, of whatever color or sex you like – and what

> you risk in being truly yourself, the way you want to be is not the loss of me. You are *not* free, however, to think I am a fool.[11]

Black people have undergone centuries of oppression and racism. The pain, trauma and suffering which accompanied it have been withstood to the point that, as a people, we can rightly claim to be survivors. Yet that survival, for black women, is threatened by the refusal of some within our communities to acknowledge the particular pain that accompanies sexual abuse. That is a painful admission to make – but one which I feel is nevertheless true. If we are to change those expectations and perceptions, it must begin with ourselves. The problems that characterise some relations between black women and some black men – those of a personal as well as a political nature – should not threaten the solidarity of our past, current or future work in struggle as people of colour. They must not continue to bog us down. The road to sorting out those problems, however, does not lie in sweeping some of their more blatant manifestations under the carpet in the vain hope that these will go away, or at the very least, that we will shut up about it. 'It is important to bear in mind,' said psychotherapist Sonia Francis, in the context of our communities' dealing with incest and child sexual abuse, 'that it's not this or that person's fault. It's everybody's fault – a whole community's fault for letting it happen.'[12]

The gap between the expectation of black women of understanding, empathy and love, and the reality which often surfaces as abuse – sexual and otherwise – needs to be addressed. If it is not, a gulf could develop between us, which might not be easily traversed. We cannot afford to let that happen. As black people who are collectively threatened by racism, we are only as strong as the weakest link. Right now the weak link, represented by the failure of some black men within our communities to address their own sexual boundary-crossing, is a glaring one.

> We need to challenge ourselves, to challenge the black community to take leadership in the caring for those of us who have been damaged by sexual assault. We need to deal with and challenge Black organizations in this community to meet the needs of those of us who have been assaulted.[13]

Outcomes

Failure to meet this challenge can mean that some black women who have been sexually abused as children may turn away from their communities entirely, and turn into themselves. This, it goes without saying, is not a desirable outcome. It involves bottling up the guilt, pain and confusion to an even greater degree. Such women may fail to recognise their worth or ability to transcend the trauma. These women are victims in a very real sense, and their loss weakens us all.

For those of us who appear to transcend the fact of our abuse, there is no support for or acknowledgement of our position. On the contrary, we are chastised when we dare to work through this trauma openly. Whether we fight it or capitulate, as women, as black women, we must be aware of the dynamics of sexist oppression and how it works to try and turn us into victims, and keep us as victims, once we become victimised.

Some insight into what the issue of incest and child sexual abuse, viewed from a black feminist perspective, can mean for black women can be gained from the following excerpt of a speech made in 1987 by Marlene Bogle, a one-time co-ordinator of the Brixton Black Women's Centre, in south London:

> What has to be understood is that what it means to have

> been abused is different for each incest survivor, dependent on their other experiences. Black women survivors have the experience of racism as a factor in the meaning for them. It was recognition of this which started the work on sexual violence at the Black Women's Centre.[14]

Family dysfunction and blaming black women

One reason why it is important to advance a black and feminist perspective in the field of child sexual abuse is because it challenges the view of the black family as dysfunctional: that it has inherent problems which are a result of its make-up and/or the dynamics within it. The dysfunction theory states that sexual abuse occurs in families with problems; problems, the theory holds, which can be caused by inadequate or unavailable mothers. It is, however, an erroneous premise (and one which should be countered) to say that CSA occurs only or even mainly in 'problem families'. One of the things we know for certain is that it occurs across the socioeconomic spectrum. It is also important to recognise that this theory represents another assault on black women and roles prescribed for us, which often do not jibe with how we see ourselves.

The work of Mary MacLeod and Esther Saraga, two feminist campaigners in the field and founders of the Child Abuse Studies Unit at the University of North London, is a good starting point for an assessment of the dysfunction argument. It helps to unpack the professional rhetoric and does much to identify the underlying reasons for it. Discussing the ease with which the dysfunctional family explanation gained acceptance, they note:

> The absence of proper public debate is not the result of a consensus; but it arises from the dominance of one particular theory according to which child sexual abuse occurs in 'dysfunctional families': that is families in which

> something has gone wrong – usually because the wife/mother has failed to fulfil her role. The literature is vociferous in its condemnation of mothers of abused children, claiming that they either actively collude in the abuse, or do nothing about it . . . Where the man's responsibility is acknowledged, he is said to be the 'victim' of the 'cycle of abuse' – that he was abused himself in childhood.
>
> The effect of these ideas is to put child sexual abuse into the realm of the 'abnormal' – something which happens when gender roles and traditional family values are not adhered to. And this often leads people to make the incorrect assumption that child sexual abuse occurs more in Black and working class families which are said to be dysfunctional. According to this argument, the 'cure' lies in the strengthening of the family.[15]

The main point to be made with regard to this theory and black people is that the criteria against which black families are judged by some professionals who contribute to the incest industry (which will be discussed in more detail later) is based firmly within a Eurocentric framework; a framework which fails to understand or even attempt to understand the complexities or the dimensions of black family life.

Patricia Hill Collins, a Black American feminist and scholar, discusses the tendency to impose Eurocentric values on non-European cultures in her essay, 'The Meaning of Motherhood in Black Culture and Black Mother/Daughter Relationships'. She refers to research by a West African sociologist, Christine Oppong, which 'suggests that the Western notion of equating household with family be abandoned because it obscures women's family roles in African cultures'. Collins notes:

> While the archetypal white, middle-class nuclear family conceptualizes family life as being divided into two oppositional spheres – the 'male' sphere of economic providing and the 'female' sphere of affective nurturing –

> this type of rigid sex role segregation was not part of the West African tradition. Mothering was not a privatized nurturing 'occupation' reserved for biological mothers, and the economic support of children was not the exclusive responsibility of men. Instead, for African women, emotional care for children and providing for their physical survival were interwoven as interdependent, complementary dimensions of motherhood.[16]

Collins points to recent research which shows that more of this traditional, African-based concept of mothering has been retained by African-Americans than had previously been thought; and that a workable variation of this West African perspective has developed in response to the pressures and changes wrought by the dominant Eurocentric American culture, to produce an Afrocentric ideology of motherhood. Similarly, in Britain, this concept holds up. Black women, upon marriage, have not expected, or been expected, to remain within the home. The economic realities of life for black people in this country, as elsewhere, has historically and to the present day made this an impracticality.

This does not suggest that the black family is harmed by, or becomes (or indeed is) dysfunctional because of this fact. Black women and black families have traditionally had to develop other means to ensure their survival in response to the pressures engendered by racism and economic disadvantage. Collins notes that one response to this was the development of 'women-centred' networks which have the responsibility of nurturing and care for children within a community-wide ethos:

> In African-American communities, the boundaries distinguishing biological mothers of children from other women who care for children are often fluid and changing. Biological mothers or bloodmothers are expected to care for their children. But African and African-American

> communities have also recognized that vesting one person with full responsibility for mothering a child may not be wise or possible. As a result, 'othermothers,' women who assist bloodmothers by sharing mothering responsibilities, traditionally have been central to the institution of Black motherhood.

Blaming women for the occurrence of child sexual abuse is not a new phenomenon. The gender twist associated with the blame of black women for its occurrence in black communities, however, cannot go unchallenged. Despite rumblings about the tip of the iceberg of female sexual abuse of children (discussed later), overwhelming evidence points to men as the primary perpetrators. No amount of theorising about its causes can escape that fact.

The issue to be addressed, instead, is that of why CSA is to be found in every stratum of society. Contained within this should be a critical discussion of why it is equally widespread in so-called 'normal' families. The questions to be asked are: 'What is normal?' and 'Whose normality?'

No doubt there are many women who have been sexually abused as children who do indeed hold their mothers responsible for what has happened to them. 'I think there are some mothers who never knew,' said one survivor, 'but *this* mother [her mother] knew. She beat me. The way she beat me told me so. Her tears told me so. It was then that I knew that she knew that I knew.'

Another mother colluded upon learning of her daughter's incest, because of the precarious nature of the family's economic circumstances, and because she could not face the prospect of life without her man. I am convinced that my own mother did not know of my abuse. This is due in part to the fact that she was not around for long periods of my childhood – being a working black woman who had to provide for her own and her children's welfare in the face of a crumbling marriage.

A cursory viewing of the situation would suggest that we fit the Western scenario ascribed to the dysfunctional family: that is, one that does not function normally because of an absent or collusive mother. But a wider view reveals, as Collins notes, the presence of 'othermothers' in our lives. The presence of such women is not unusual in black communities. Rather, they are an integral and expected part of our cultural tradition. In my case, there was my grandmother, who also was not aware of the abuse, but who provided the stability that I needed in an otherwise precarious world. Other survivors have spoken of aunts or mother's friends or other women who took them under their wing.

The starting point for why sexual abuse occurs, however, should not be where the mother *was*, but what the father or male *did*. Cultural considerations which should more appropriately be taken into account include the effects of poverty and economic circumstances. Though it is no defence for the perpetration of CSA it is important to note the part played by poverty. Writing within the context of Asian mothers and their families Researcher Melody Mtezuka noted in her study:

> They insisted that poverty played a large part in persuading female members to keep the abuse secret. Thus if the perpetrator was the breadwinner, exposure might break up a family which shouldered a considerable number of responsibilities, not only for the extended family members in this country, but also for some of those relatives still living abroad.[17]

She adds that this did not mean that family members condoned the abuse; but all, including the abused girl, were trapped in an oppressive set of circumstances and a tragedy brought on largely by the disadvantages faced by minority groups in the UK.

While I agree with Mtezuka's analysis of economic disadvantage caused by racism, which applies to many black people in Western societies, I do not accept that economic disadvantage is the *cause* of child sexual abuse in black communities. Sexual abuse happens because men want it to happen; and they will use any excuse, including the consequences of being denied full economic participation in order to justify it.

This does not discount the fact that many women who are sexually abused as children do, indeed blame their mothers. Nor does it deny that some mothers do collude in their children's abuse – feminist theory has never sought to deny either of these viewpoints. But, as Pat Agana notes, the theory surrounding family dysfunction as it relates to black people, *begins* by blaming the mother. Its precept is to assign to the mother an 'all-seeing, all-knowing, all-caring' nature, says Agana. The difference between survivors blaming their mothers and the family dysfunction theory which holds them ultimately responsible, however, is vast. One is a consequence of the process which a child, any child, will go through in order to sort out the confusion about the abuse. The other is a deliberate political process whose starting point is an attempt to get men, who, it has been shown, are overwhelmingly abusers of children, off the hook.

Pioneering feminist writer Sarah Nelson, in her book, *Incest: Fact and Myth*, had this to say about the commission of incest by men:

> Incest is related to a general pattern of male sexual assaults like rape. Much of this is culturally sanctioned or not taken seriously by society, and most assaults are never reported. Incest is also a product of family structure; but the clue lies in normal family values, not deviant ones. Like wife beating, incest is likely to happen when traditional beliefs about the roles of husband, wife and daughter are taken to extremes; when the family members are seen as the

husband's property, and sex is among the services they are expected to provide.[18]

Cultural differences

Another reason for developing a black and feminist perspective about CSA concerns the need to look at cultural differences in how sexual abuse is manifested in black communities. This involves an examination of our experiences of abuse (what actually happens) and in how we choose to deal with them as black people (for example, there is often a reluctance to go to the authorities). We need to look at life experiences: for example, growing up poor and black in Texas, instead of white and middle class in wherever; or at specific instances: for example, at who perpetrates sexual abuse. Research has shown that a significant proportion of black girls are abused by their mother's men friends.[19] What are the implications of *that* in our communities?

In 'A Comparison of Afro-American and White American Victims', Russell et al. note:

> That the experiences of white victims are assumed to be the norm for all minority victims is evident in the lack of ethnicity-based child sexual abuse research. But the assumption that data on Whites accurately reflect the experiences of the members of all other groups denies the role of cultural differences in people's lives, denies the fact that racism has an impact, and reflects the White bias of most researchers in this field.[20]

In practice, it has meant that child sexual abuse has come to be regarded, as Marlene Bogle and others have pointed out, as the norm by some within and many outside black communities. In addition, ignorance of or a refusal to accept the existence of sexual abuse as an issue in non-white communities has had the effect of obstructing or limiting access to treatment for many black children who are abused.

The following account from a 1984 New York Women Against Rape conference was related by Julia Perez, a black, Puerto Rican social worker and organiser. It illustrates the pitfalls inherent in adhering to stereotypes. The incident, she said, involved 'four white men, a white feminist and a Jewish woman':

> I walked into the room . . . One of the young men, because he knows I work with men in prison, said to me, 'I am doing a survey to see what kind of a sentence you would give a man who raped, and has been sexually molesting his six-year-old daughter.' I said: 'I would put his ass in jail, for life.' This woman looked up at me and said, 'Well honey, you might as well put all your Black brothers down South in prison because this is a socially acceptable mode of behavior among Blacks there.' I just looked at her and said, 'Where did you get your statistics?' I didn't drag her out because I didn't have the energy to do that.
>
> I walked out into the hall with this knot in my stomach and pain that you could not believe. Then, the feminist walked out and said, 'That's really terrible she did that to you, because we all know that Black families are female-headed anyway.'[21]

The message of black feminists must be twofold. First, to make clear that black women and children do not expect to be sexually abused as a matter of course. We must stress that, if we are to survive as whole and healthy communities, we cannot allow some of our men to continue to carry out this abuse, and remain silent about it. It is a position based on the inalienable right we have as women to complete and undisputed control over our bodies.

The black feminist position as regards child sexual abuse is one of challenging aggressive and oppressive male behaviour on the basis that it violates our rights as women and as black people. There's a line in the film, *The Color Purple,* in which Celie, when freeing herself from the oppressive presence of Mister tells him, 'Whatever you've done to me has already been done to you.' Black men (and black women) who view feminism as a 'white girl's thing' and who regard the struggle of black feminists as secondary and far to the back of the black struggle would do well to remember that it is only when we all 'reach the promised land' as whole, healthy human beings, that our people really will be free. We cannot continue to trash one half of the body politic and expect the repercussions not to rebound on all of us as people of colour.

Black feminism must also speak to those outside our communities, about their stereotypes of black women and black men. For it is only by gaining an understanding of the ways in which we as black people and as women are oppressed by existing power structures (which an exploration of feminism affords), that we can begin to change our destinies and take control of our lives. The following excerpt, written two years ago by a black woman involved with the London Rape Crisis Centre, says a great deal about how far the distance to be travelled is:

> The London Rape Crisis Centre has a long history of difficulties with providing a service for Black and Ethnic Minority women, either within the Centre itself and with women who use the service. These difficulties came about through the Centre's refusal to acknowledge certain issues around rape/sexual assault for Black women . . . The Centre's analysis of rape had only been seen from an able-bodied white middle class perspective. Racism and other forms of oppression of women have not been seriously taken on by the Centre. It has only been in recent years that Black women who use the line can have Black counsellors – The Centre's philosophy of 'rape is the abuse of power by men and that all women can talk to each other about rape' had made it easy for white women to go no further in their

> analysis to look at other forms of oppression of women. Thus, in the case of Black women, the analysis denied the power imbalance between white and black women and the issue of racism within the Centre.[22]

During the 1980s the case which black feminists made for autonomous organising was a strong one, and one whose validity remains. The racism we encountered in the women's movement, for example, reflected a reluctance to move beyond stereotypes about black people, or to embrace a world view anything other than Eurocentric. It accounted for the move of black women away from that movement and towards the positive ethos engendered through black women coming together with common ground beneath us. Because of the conjunction of sexism and racism, as far as child sexual abuse and incest in black communities are concerned, the primacy of the case for autonomous organising remains.

Women as abusers

In recent years, reports in the media have tended to advance the 'tip of the iceberg' theory to suggest that there is widespread sexual abuse of children by women; abuse which goes undetected and unreported. At a recent conference in London, the first of its kind to look at the incidence of women sexually abusing children, Michele Elliott, respected campaigner against child sexual abuse and a declared feminist, began by saying that the issue of women as sexual abusers of children 'was not one which she went out to look for'.

Elliott noted that, as a feminist, she found it a very painful subject with which to deal, but that approach it she must because of the unavoidable evidence from adult survivors – male and female – who were coming forward to declare that they had been abused as children by their mothers, aunts, grandmothers or babysitters.

She likened the resistance, among feminists especially, to accepting the fact of sexual abuse by women, to that encountered when the whole issue of child sexual abuse was raised in earnest more than a decade ago. Then, as now, reporting of such abuse was met with general disbelief and a refusal to accept that there was anything like the amount of it that we now know exists, said Elliott. But, citing the 127 people who contacted Kidscape, the charity of which she is director, with their stories of abuse by women, the fact of women's abuse of children is inescapable; but society owes it to the survivors, not to mention children who are still being abused, to investigate.[23]

Why women abuse

A number of explanations about why women may sexually abuse children emerged during the conference. One was to the effect that 'it was a bit of harmless fun'. Elliott noted that the uproar would have been immense if reported abuse by men, when its incidence began to be made known, had been met with a similar reaction. Why, she wanted to know, should sexual abuse by women be less problematic than that by men? Other explanations were that it constituted a way of teaching the abused the ropes; or that women who abused were coerced into doing it by the men in their lives.

American psychologist Jane Matthews, a conference participant, has worked extensively with female sexual abusers in a Minnesota sex offender treatment programme for women and is a co-author of one of the very few studies on female sex offenders.[24] She reported on her research based on work carried out initially with sixteen women in the Genesis II programme for women, a private, non-profit, community corrections agency in Minneapolis. Matthews has identified three categories of female sexual offenders: the teacher/lover; the predisposed (inter-generational) and the male-coerced. The categories, said Matthews, represented a cluster of attributes which pertained to the crimes the women committed, their perceptions of the victims, the involvement of co-offenders and psychological similarities and differences.

The teacher/lover, according to Matthews's study, 'is generally involved with prepubescent and adolescent males with whom she relates as a peer'. Her motive is 'to teach her young victims about sexuality'. Far from the commonly held view of some that such an initiation is everybody's dream, noted Matthews, the reality for boys 'broken in' in this way is shame and feelings of having been taken advantage of, which results in a high incidence of suicide attempts.

The predisposed female sexual abuser, according to Matthews, is usually herself a victim of severe sexual abuse, which has been initiated at a very young age and has persisted over a long period of time. Matthews's findings indicate that 'she initiates the sexual abuse herself, and her victims are her own children. Her motive is to achieve non-threatening emotional intimacy.' She is also said to be self-loathing, very dependent and plagued by emotional turmoil.

The male-coerced female sexual abuser is said to act initially in conjunction with a male who has abused children. She exhibits a pattern of extreme dependency on males, is non-assertive, yet full of anger about what she sees as her passive female role, and may eventually initiate sexual abuse herself. Matthews describes this type of female abuser as the 'Tammy Wynette/Stand By Your Man' syndrome.

Another study of thirty-six female sexual offenders, carried out by Matthews, included three black women. All were in the predisposed category and, according to Matthews, there were no significant differences between them and their white counterparts.

Who commits sexual abuse?

Notwithstanding the 127 people who contacted Michele Elliott's Kidscape with their stories of sexual abuse by women, or the women who make up Jane Matthews's study, it becomes important to place any discussion about who perpetrates sexual abuse within the context of what the wide body of evidence tells us about its occurrence – that in the overwhelming majority of reported instances it is men who sexually abuse children. The feminist response to reportings of sexual abuse by women, though it does not seek to deny its occurrence (on the contrary, it was feminists operating within a context of openness and open-mindedness about sexual abuse who helped to uncover its true incidence, among men as well as women) is rightly wary of the inordinate attention paid in recent years to uncovering sexual abuse by women.

Liz Kelly, feminist campaigner and activist around issues of CSA, as part of her work with the Child Abuse Studies Unit (CASU) at the University of North London noted that:

> The information we have about women who sexually abuse is extremely limited, in part because they are much fewer in number, and because we currently lack the rich insight of survivors' accounts.
>
> Most published studies reveal that some three per cent of adult sexual abusers are women. The NSPCC, in a section of their 1990 national report which was not picked up by the media, stated categorically that their figures did not support the popular 'tip of the iceberg' view of women as abusers.[25]

A 1991 CASU study found that 'the vast majority of abuse was committed by men'. The study surveyed 1,244 young people (777 women and 467 men) aged between 16 and 21 on the prevalence of sexual abuse. The findings indicated a 59 per cent prevalence rate for women who had been abused and a 27 per cent rate for men. The figures for who carried out the abuse were women 8 per cent, and men 92 per cent.

Information obtained from the National Society for the Prevention of Cruelty to Children on the years 1983–7 includes a breakdown of suspected perpetrators from a sampling of 1,445 cases of sexual abuse reported to local authorities.

The person suspected of perpetrating the abuse was recorded for 94 per cent of cases. The findings included the following figures: number of natural mothers committing abuse (24), number of natural fathers committing abuse (490); stepmother (0), stepfather (231); mother substitute (1), father substitute (164).[26]

A National Children's Home/Department of Health survey of treatment facilities for young sexual abusers of children (1990) indicated that 'the majority of those with whom work was undertaken were males aged between 15 and 17 . . . virtually no female abusers were reported to be seen by any facility in the NCH/DoH survey'.[27]

Many of us, particularly those who are survivors of male sexual abuse, regard the attentiveness to incidence of sexual abuse by females, as another attempt to get men off the hook. It has the feel of a dangerous smokescreen, which could divert attention from the overwhelming evidence of widespread abuse by men, and effectively put more children at risk of abuse. It is difficult to believe, for example, that with the widespread attention the issue of child sexual abuse has received in the past ten years there are countless numbers of people out there who have not come forward to name their female abusers. I simply cannot believe that, given our society's quickness off the mark to oppress and downgrade women, this is an issue which would not have surfaced to a greater extent than has so far been exhibited.

Michele Elliott admits that her figures might point to the tip of the iceberg or it may be '*the* iceberg'. I would argue that it is more likely to be the latter. The male psyche, as it tries to squirm out of the line of fire of responsibility from what is essentially an indefensible position of aggressive sexuality would, I think, stop at nothing to try and shift the harsh glare of scrutiny. In that I would include attempts to shift the spotlight on to the so-called tip of the iceberg of abuse by women.

Black women and abuse

As noted earlier, Jane Matthews's study uncovered three black women sexual abusers of children. The study by Gail Wyatt, which compared the sexual abuse of Afro-American and white American women in childhood found four black female perpetrators out of 147 incidents reported by Afro-American women (see note 20). It is impossible to calculate from this what the actual numbers may be, and far be it from me to do so. None of the women with whom I spoke, and whose experiences form part of this book, were sexually abused by their mothers. However, the issue of abuse by black women did come up in conversations. This most often took the form of physical and/or emotional abuse by black mothers, an issue which surfaces again and again in conversations with black women generally.

One black woman survivor I spoke to had this to say about the emotional abuse to which some black women subject their children:

> Emotional abuse is as bad as sexual abuse. With sexual abuse people at least can see forensic evidence. But emotional abuse occurs with every form of abuse, and it is less provable. You

> can't have physical or sexual abuse without emotional abuse. The pain an individual carries as a result of being unloved or untalented is not acknowledged; and even if it is, if people don't actually hear what you're saying it can be worse. I think black women abuse emotionally and physically, but not sexually. Black women also abuse through neglect, usually because of mental illness.

In addition, the inability or refusal of some black mothers (whether because of economic and/or emotional dependency upon their male partners) to act upon the fact of a child's disclosed or suspected sexual abuse undoubtedly causes real and ingrained pain for black women survivors of incest:

> I remember my mom slept with me one night. I used to have dreams that I was falling down into a pit. My mom kept asking me what was wrong. I told her I wanted to die. She moved away from me at that point in bed. I remember her emotionally moving away as well and I've never been able to reach her since. My mother did know.

> When I was 18, I talked to my mom one day about it all. We had a big row. She ripped all my clothes off – down to my bra. She was scratching and clawing at me. I went to hit her back and my brother, who was 13, beat me up. That finished the relationship with everybody in the house. They all had this view of me as a whore.

Part of the pain of surviving for many of us comes from the fact that it is difficult to reconcile the position of our mothers, if we felt they knew, with our fears about their reactions.

One survivor raised a number of questions about women who may abuse, within the context of black female survivors and their adult response to their own abuse. A social worker, she noted that 'in social work, we learn that if a male is abusing, nine out of ten times he was abused when young.

But you never really see black women sexual abusers. But how are we working out those feelings of the abuse? Are we talking about it? Are we being over-protective of our children? Are we abusing our children?'

Many questions, few answers. Certainly many black women have a job cut out for them in overcoming the stereotype (widely held) that we are harsh and unable to display real love and affection towards our children and black men. A situation which is perhaps explained, to some extent, by the survival techniques which black women had to adopt under slavery and which have had to be honed in successive aspects of a colonial existence.

It must also be borne in mind that many black women do prevent abuse; and that they do not emotionally or physically abuse. The anecdotal and statistical evidence I have been able to uncover so far does not add up to the existence of widespread sexual abuse by black women.

There does appear to be a need for a closer examination of emotional and/or physical abuse by some black mothers. Many black women survivors and non-survivors alike have raised this as an issue for black communities. In this regard, I commend what bell hooks had to say about the 'transformational politic' which feminism, and black feminism in particular, can offer:

> Clearly, differentiation between strong and weak, powerful and powerless, has been a central defining aspect of gender globally, carrying with it the assumption that men should have greater authority than women, and should rule over them. As significant and important as this fact is, it should not obscure the reality that women can and do participate in politics of domination, as perpetrators as well as victims – that we dominate, that we are dominated . . . thinking speculatively about early human social arrangement, about women and men struggling to survive in small communities, it is likely that the parent–child relationship with its very real imposed survival structure of dependency, of strong

> and weak, of powerful and powerless, was a site for the construction of a paradigm of domination . . . Right now as I speak, a man who is himself victimized, wounded, hurt by racism and class exploitation is actively dominating a woman in his life – that even as I speak, women who are ourselves exploited, victimized, are dominating children. It is necessary for us to remember, as we think critically about domination, that we all have the capacity to act in ways that oppress, dominate, wound (whether or not the power is institutionalized). It is necessary to remember that it is first the potential oppressor within that we must resist – the potential victim within that we must rescue – otherwise we cannot hope for an end to domination, for liberation.[28]

It seems to me that hooks's words have particular relevance in the sphere of female abuse, be it sexual or otherwise. As black women and black people, we would do well to take such words to heart in an effort to overcome the beasts within all of us which would hurt and harm in the interests of domination.

Men, women and child sexual abuse

One of the most compelling explanations I have yet come across for why men commit sexual abuse against children is discussed by noted sexual abuse researcher, David Finkelhor.[29] Finkelhor outlined several key differences between women and men regarding their socialisation processes which, I feel, speak to the heart of the matter in helping to explain underlying reasons why men commit child sexual abuse. He also goes some way towards putting the issue of sexual abuse by women into a more realistic perspective. Among the crucial differences identified by Finkelhor are the following:

(1) **Women learn earlier and much more completely to distinguish between sexual and non-sexual forms of affection** According to Finkelhor, men are not given as

many legitimate opportunities (for example through preparation for motherhood) to practise nurturing and to express dependency needs except through sex – so that when men need affection and are feeling dependent they are much more likely to look for fulfilment in a sexual form, even with an inappropriate partner. Women, he notes, can also get such needs met with children, but without sexualising the relationship.

(2) **Men grow up seeing heterosexual success as much more important to their gender identities than women do** When their egos or their competencies suffer any insult, men are much more likely than women to feel a need for sex as a way of reconfirming their adequacy, even if the only easily available sexual partner is a child. Sex with children, notes Finkelhor, may be a weak confirmation, but it is some confirmation.

(3) **Men are socialised to be able to focus their sexual interest around sexual acts isolated from the context of a relationship** Women, by contrast, are taught to focus on whole romantic contexts and whole relationships. The ability of men to relate concretely to sexual acts, says Finkelhor, is illustrated in their greater ability to be aroused by children. For women, the fact that a partner was a child would make it more difficult to experience sexual interest in that partner. Men, however, could experience arousal because the partner, even though a child, had the right kind of genitals or could engage in the desired sex act.

(4) **Finally, men are socialised to see as their appropriate sexual partners persons who are younger and smaller than themselves, while women are socialised to see as their appropriate sexual partners persons older and larger** It is easier, notes Finkelhor, for a man to find a child sexually attractive because children are merely an extension of the gradient along which his appetites are already focused.

Finkelhor points out that it 'is not simply a matter of abuse by women going undetected, since even in nonclinical surveys of adults reporting retrospectively on childhood sexual experiences, the male perpetrators vastly outnumbered the women'.[30]

In 1984, following collaborative work with Diana Russell, Finkelhor said:

> After reviewing all the studies, Diana Russell and I conclude . . . that men constitute 95 per cent of the perpetrators in cases of abuse of girls and 80 per cent in cases of abuse of boys.[31]

Inappropriate sexual behaviour by men is borne out by the stories told to me. One survivor said: 'My dad was always getting thrown out of the bedroom. He used to keep pornographic material around the house. He had stuff that said things like: "If your daughter doesn't love you – you could sex her."'

Whatever the manifestation of the abuse, it is possible to see links between the behaviour and the theory. This does not diminish the feelings of violation, but it does go some way in helping to frame an understanding of the frequently asked question: 'Why did it have to happen to me?' If we can begin to put the answer to that question into some kind of workable context, out of this may come a construct, grounded in an understanding of the male socialisation process (which feminist and other theories provide). The complexity of our abuse can begin to be unravelled and put behind us.

CHAPTER 6

Success, survival and the professional incest industry

> I decided that part of my life was over; so I wanted to achieve something. I studied hard; got an excellent degree and felt, right: 'If I can't be good in one way, then I'll be good at something else.' But deep down, it doesn't get better and the more you suppress it, the worse it gets. (Black woman survivor)

It is not for nothing that we black women have an image of being strong and powerful – we are. Well, we are and we aren't. The woman who spoke the words above felt very strong on one level – she had achieved. She had got herself an 'excellent degree', and a good job. She was a success. She was her own woman, and she did it all in spite of experiencing deep trauma about being sexually abused as a young girl. No problem, right. Black women can take it all. We can be knocked down, kicked around, fucked and fucked over as children and as adults, and we bounce right back, taking it all in our stride; landing on our feet in time to fend off the next barrage. Right?

Wrong. The speaker above was an incest survivor who had, indeed, outwardly put the incest behind her. She represents, for many black women, one of the main dilemmas for us in choosing to make public the fact of our sexual abuse as children. On the one hand, many of us are successful – academically, career-wise, financially – to varying degrees: we snapped out of it and got on with our lives.

We've done what was expected of us as strong black women, who are used to taking it on the chin. One almost has the feeling that the view within our communities is that our ability to withstand the trauma of childhood sexual abuse is considered a piece of cake in comparison to the 'larger', historical ravages of slavery, economic exploitation, rape and the wrenching apart of black families. There is an unspoken as well as spoken epithet that we shouldn't make a fuss, especially at this late date in our lives. The view is that we should just put it all behind us; chalk it up to experience; and be glad that we're still alive to tell the tale.

Well, no. It doesn't exactly work that way. At least not from where I'm sitting as a survivor. Thirty-two years after the sexual involvement with my father, and varying degrees of success in what I've chosen to do in life, I still felt (overwhelmingly) the urge to write this book – to put down my feelings, to try and encourage other black women whom I know to be in broadly similar situations to do the same. All of us want to try to make sense of why it had to happen to us – and yes, even after many years, we *are* still trying to make some sense of it, despite the fact that some of us may not remember the abuse.

> I find that people who have been abused and put it behind them excel in other ways. But they don't want to look at the abuse or even more important, their feelings about it. It normally comes out in relationships – for instance, a pattern develops, like not being able to have a stable relationship. I went through a stage when I did not want to be with a black man. If I liked a black man, I made a lot of assumptions about what he could or couldn't do – like black men couldn't be romantic, warm or expressive.

I am not suggesting that as black women who have survived incest and who, hopefully, *have* gone on to become successes, we want to wallow in our abuse; or to let it define who we are as people and as women. The time has come, however, to stop acquiescing in the silence surrounding it; to stop pretending it didn't happen; to discard the reasoning that we shouldn't make a fuss and thereby make our families and/or communities look bad.

It is now time to begin a dialogue about sexual abuse in black communities. Yes, many of us are successful. We have learned to live with and in spite of, our abuse as children (if we're lucky, that is; the unlucky ones cannot tell their stories). The fact that we can do this is a testament to our strength and survival skills; *but it does not wipe the slate clean.*

Therein lies the heart of the matter. Many of us are successful, yet we have pain. We are committed to our families/communities, yet equally, we want those families/communities to allow us the space we need. This is the very least that we deserve. That space is vital so that we may face and assess what it is that prevents some of us from moving on, as whole, complete human beings. And, yes, many of us have survived, but at what cost? The answer, for some, is that it has been at the expense of a sense of emotional well-being; of being able to feel good about ourselves. For others, it is a more visible cost – self-mutilation, or even suicide.

One survivor put it this way:

> I think black women have had a hard time. Black men think black women should be strong. We're supposed to be strong and long-suffering. We're supposed to be tough, and able to work through things and get on with things. We are not supposed to be vulnerable or weak. I know what the image of a black woman is supposed to be. I've been through it – but I cry easily. And I think: I'm a big, strong black woman; and when I cry, people get two messages. I hope you tell

> people that it's OK to be vulnerable sometimes. That it's OK to have that space.

Forcing the issue – by labelling and dealing with our own vulnerability – is yet another way in which we can begin to challenge the stereotyped view as it hinders our deliberations about ourselves. When we say: 'I am vulnerable, because this thing happened to me. I am vulnerable in ways which I may not even be aware; vulnerable in spite of my success', we can help to facilitate getting a dialogue started about child abuse, and in this way get on to black people's agendas.

We can focus the discussion. We can inform the debate. We can start in our own families. In the course of researching and writing this I have spoken to members of my own family, who have a range of mixed emotions about the book. One of my nephews, who is now adult, was unaware of what had happened with me and my father until his mother told him about the book. I had heard, through the family grapevine, that he was upset about it, and was wondering why I had to bring it all up now.

He rang me one day and asked if he could discuss it with me. 'I don't even know where to begin, Auntie Melba,' he said. 'I didn't know all of that was happening. I don't even know *what* happened.' I told him in broad terms about the incest. I told him that when I was a young girl there had been an intimacy between me and his papa (grandfather); and that it had not been an appropriate closeness for a young girl to have had with her father. I told him that it was something that had stayed with me, and bothered me all my life, and that I felt it was time to finally bring it out in the open. I told him that it wasn't my intention to hurt the family, but that it was something I no longer wanted to pretend didn't happen; that I no longer wanted to cover it up any more. It was part of me, part of my life experience. That it was important to talk about it in this way because if another daddy or uncle or papa was abusing a child, and someone who knew about it heard what I had to say, then maybe, just maybe, they might decide to do something about it.

He listened quietly, without comment. He didn't say very much after I'd told him, except that he guessed I had to do what I felt was right. I felt better for having told him, though I have to admit that I was more than a little nervous about his reaction. But we got beyond that point, and I hope that in the process he gained an awareness that sexual abuse happens to real people, to people we all know. He now knows something of the effect. It is in his consciousness, as a young black man. That's important, because one day he may be in a position to prevent abuse, or at least to recognise or acknowledge its occurrence.

If this dialogue is to begin, it must, should, start one-to-one in families, and spread outward. The quiet, but persistent message is that first, the whole question of sex and sexuality should be addressed openly; and second, within that, the discussion about incest and child sexual abuse should begin as a matter of urgency.

> After the breakup of my first marriage, I was a single parent, a working adult and enjoying a measure of success, yet the mountain [of abuse] was still in control. My sense of worth was steadily diminishing; nothing covered my deep sense of shame. The 'filth' of my secret was eating me up and there was no one to confide in. I desired intimacy, but I was afraid to allow anyone male or female, to come close to knowing me. I had no experience in relating in honest relationships. The demands that I placed on myself to 'be perfect' did not allow for leisure, nor did I have the patience with others who wouldn't or couldn't measure up to my specifications.[1]

What price survival and success?

What looks like success is not always. We survive the incest, if we're lucky, but the scars remain. One survivor described living with the scars in this way: 'Once you break your leg, it's broken – but it can mend. With sexual abuse, it's like you're limping for the rest of your life. One day I just decided I had to stop and deal with it.'

The women who are counselled by psychotherapist Sonia Francis, who practises in Brixton, south London, range in age from 22 to 42. Most are self-referrals. Some are suicidally depressed, says Francis. They had good jobs and good prospects but were not happy. Some were not fulfilling their potential. Some had double degrees, but were not able to get on in life. Others had problems relating to men. Still others may have had a crisis from which they were unable to recover. The crack can show itself in a number of ways – through failed relationships; unexpected and untimely road-blocks in our careers, which inexplicably we find ourselves unable to manage; or complete breakdown.

Relationships

Many black women who survive incest, in the physical sense, do so at the expense of their emotional selves. We juggle our success and our survival – sometimes able to blank out the pain, at other times dropping the ball.

> At first, I went around feeling I was persecuted. I see most things that men do as abuse – so I always have to keep pulling back and keeping things in perspective. For example, with making love. Once my partner moved my leg over in the middle of it and I was really upset that he handled me in that way. I had to work through all of that in the middle of making love. At one point I couldn't make love for two years because I would seize up.
>
> I went into therapy when I was 32 because I was unable

> to make love. I was getting flashbacks to the abuse during lovemaking and it got worse and worse. It would start all fine and seem to be going somewhere, and then it wouldn't happen.
>
> I have a son. I had a good relationship with his father, but we broke up because I couldn't have sex. I felt scornful about the sperm. It was all this wet stuff. After we broke up, I kept saying to people: 'But we really like each other.' We did like each other and we could have lived together if he hadn't wanted sex. It got to the point where I kept looking for things to be wrong with him, so that we would break up and then I wouldn't have to have sex. This didn't do much for his self-esteem.

Another survivor said:

> I can remember that I couldn't stand my son's maleness. I also have a daughter. My son babysits sometimes and I find myself wondering what happens when they're together.
>
> My daughter also spends time with her father at weekends. At one point she didn't want to go and I began to feel that he must be abusing her. It turned out that he wasn't.
>
> With my son I had to give myself homework: my homework was to hug this boy every day – no matter what. It was physical – the fact that I didn't want to be close to him and yet, I need to be close to him. It took me about three or four years to work it through. Now he's coming up to 16 and it's OK.
>
> I have to re-frame everything when it comes to men, because my instinctive reaction is mistrust.

Work

For many women who survive incest, there is a very real sense of urgency to get through all of this stuff. The urgency lies in the fact that though we may appear confident, though we may be very capable, though we may have a certain gift to do something – if, underneath it all we are stymied by the incest, then any success is illusory.

> Right now, I'm not working. I haven't worked for the last five years. My last official job finished then. I am a fashion designer – hats, coats, wedding dresses. I work from home. Two years ago I went to work for a woman as a sample machinist. During that time I was being beaten up [by partner] and I couldn't concentrate. I just told her I couldn't cope and stopped work. I've had no full-time work since.
>
> For the past two or three years, I've been trying to find work. I don't want to go back into the fashion world because it's so superficial. I'm not into the beauty industry and the European thing any longer. I want to do something around therapy.
>
> I've got no self-confidence. For example, I make trousers. It should take about an hour, maximum to make a pair. But, I go to do it, and then I start to feel that I can't do it, that it's too much. Wedding dresses are horrific.
>
> It's because of the incest. I always felt that I'd never do well in life, afterwards. When I was going through college, I could never imagine myself as a fashion designer; and that's exactly what's happened.
>
> I couldn't imagine being happy because I was such a bad person; and I felt that in relationships people would find out how bad I was. I tend to block off in relationships – unless they're abusive.

Emotional psyche

The urgency comes because many of us are holding on precariously. It may not even be a constant situation, or something of which we are aware. But all of a sudden something happens and we snap. We fail to connect; or we just can't see a way out of things, where we might normally be expected to.

This is a plea for space – on behalf of all of us black women who have felt distanced from ourselves and our loved ones because of the abuse perpetrated against us. It is made on behalf of those who have been disillusioned by the hypocrisy we have found in some of our families and communities; for those who have grappled with guilt, recrimination and self-blame; for those who have questioned their sexuality, integrity and honesty. Such space is no more (or less) than any wounded psyche would require. It stems from a need deep within to look at our abuse. In so doing, we can begin the essential repair of the emotional damage which results from the silence about incest.

It may seem to some, at first glance, to be making an issue where there is none. But consider, if you will, the position within which black incest survivors find themselves – abused, yet discouraged (actively at times) from even mentioning the abuse; confused, yet unable to quite figure out the reasons for the confusion; pained, yet not encouraged to explore the cause of the pain openly and honestly. The question must be asked: just what are we supposed to do with all this stuff?

The collective unease that black women survivors endure needs shifting. It should be replaced by a willingness to engage with others to gain the solace and understanding which we need. Continuing to play the role of superwoman will lead only to a reduced shelf life. Though we may appear to be superwomen, many of us retain the abused child within us. In many of us that child is fighting to give voice to the hurt that has often found no outlet, and that has become a silenced part of us. It is a silence which traps the hurt inside, where it festers and, at times, threatens to overwhelm us.

> I can remember being abused from five years old. Then, I went away for a year. I was six years old when it started again, after I came back to England. It was always the men in my mother's life. I didn't tell anyone. I used to write. I used to tell the pages, and then burn them. Teachers knew things were wrong, but didn't know what to do. I was the eldest of five children. A child who has the responsibility of a mother at age 10, and who has the sexual maturity of a woman, suffers emotional abuse. I always hoped someone

> would see – but they didn't. I always knew it was happening to a sister of mine. When I told my mother a few years ago, she didn't believe me, until my sister confirmed it. Then she was cross, because she had to talk about it.

Talking about sex makes many in our communities uncomfortable. We don't like to deal with it out in the open. We feel foolish, uncertain, about discussing our most personal feelings and desires – why not just act on them, without all this talk? Many of us think the 'S-word' should remain within the bedroom behind closed doors, under wraps. The problem for those of us black women who were victimised by sexual abuse as children, however, is precisely that it did remain under wraps. We were abused and no one knew about it, certainly didn't talk about it. If they did, it was along the lines of: 'Go away, girl, and pull yourself together.' We suffered, some of us terribly, and people said: 'We don't want to hear or know.' We faltered and fell, and people said: 'You're weak.' 'My mother told me I shouldn't speak about the incest because my dad would go to prison and she couldn't cope with five children on her own.'

The dilemmas we face are real, and not of our own choosing:

> I teach a class in self awareness for women. There was one woman (in her late 20s) who came every week; and every week she would burst into tears. She never participated. She was inconsolable and very distressed. Each time she tried to talk, there would be more tears.
>
> One of the first things she said was: 'I can't tell anybody. It's horrible. It's the most horrible thing in the whole world. And the worst part of it is that my son lives with them [parents]. What's going to happen to him?
>
> One day the other women in the class challenged her and she finally told what the problem was. It turned out that she had just remembered her father had sexually abused her. What came out was that she hated her father and mother

because no one had protected her. She hadn't remembered this until she started coming to the class.

At that point, six other women disclosed at the same time. Some felt worse about it than others; some had come to terms with it. Every person felt it was their fault – even those who had come to terms with it.

Negotiating the professional incest industry

> All he wanted was to hear what my Dad did and get turned on by it; so I shut up . . . wasn't going to tell him anything.[2]

Several years ago, about a hundred women – black and white – met to discuss sexual abuse in childhood as it affected their lives; as it affected the lives of those around them; as it is perceived by the public; and as it is dealt with by the professionals who intervene to treat or counsel women and children who have been abused. The conference united around one theme in particular – the need to reclaim the impetus for the way sexual abuse is responded to away from those professionals who have managed to create a whole industry out of the trauma of child abuse.

Not long after this conference, another similar one was held – this time for black women survivors of child sexual abuse. Again, there was common cause in uniting around the idea that as survivors, black survivors in particular, it was incumbent upon us to contribute, in a major way, to the debate about what kind of counselling should and should not be undertaken, who should and should not carry it out, and with what ends in mind. In short, there was a broad feeling that we needed to advance a general framework as survivors. There was agreement that there was merit in one survivor helping another survivor to work through the trauma, from a shared perspective.

This view is not always supported by the professional

establishment. 'The current moves towards professionalism,' notes Liz Kelly, 'involve a questioning of the experience of survivors, and of professionals who are survivors using this as a resource in their work. I detect a very strong retreat in the field. Many women now fear that if they say they are survivors, they run the risk of being taken off such cases and of being told they are too subjective or too personal. Much of the criticism of the personal comes from white, male professionals.'[3]

Pat Agana, one of the organisers of the black women's conference, told those assembled: 'It's important to get together and start to look at how we feel about child sexual abuse, because many decisions were being taken [in the fields of child abuse and child protection] without our consent.' It was, said Agana, 'a poignant area', which required that black women pool their views and experiences in order to present a constructive and coherent strategy which speaks to the particular experiences we bring as survivors.[4]

Many survivors of child sexual abuse and incest believe often another survivor is uniquely able to help ease the pain and trauma that can result from being abused (or at the very least provide an empathetic ear), in a way that a detached professional may be unwilling or unable to. There is a suspicion (not altogether unfounded) among survivors of the trend towards textbook solutions to abuse: programmes of treatment and counselling espoused, in the main, by white male professionals. Textbook solutions contribute to the Incest Industry – academic papers, conferences, surveys. (Not much on black women, though.)

Feminist writer Louise Armstrong described the effect of the incest industry in responding to the experiences of survivors of child sexual abuse:

> It was not the forces of repression that were sent to meet

> us. It was battalions of newly minted mental health professionals. And they were so sure we were *not* wrong about the incidence, and so sure we were *not* wrong about the entrenched license, that they were willing to stake their careers on it: to enter a new specialty, 'incest expert.' We had agitated the public. They believed that they had the balm to peddle which would calm them. Being professionals, they banked on the fact that their calm-balm would prevail over our call for social change. They were right. Almost from the start, the media carried our stories – and their analysis. Minutes after first opening our mouths, our message was first muffled, then obliterated.[5]

The situation for black women, however, is different again. First, much of the material which is gathered, reported on and analysed concerns white survivors of child sexual abuse. Very little has been written about the black woman's experience of incest and child sexual abuse, by comparison. (The notable exception, as I said earlier, comes in the work of black women writers, whose treatment of the subject, welcome though it is, in the main falls under the heading of literature, and not therapeutic/academic analysis as such.) The consequence is that black women survivors have seldom seen their experiences reflected and analysed in a way that is useful or beneficial to them. One psychologist with whom I spoke, a black woman, lamented the fact that when black women came to her for help, there was nothing she could show them or point them to which could help them work through their particular trauma as black women survivors.

The second issue that is problematic for black women, and which is a consequence of the professional stranglehold of the Incest Industry, concerns the fact that the experiences of white survivors are, as noted earlier, automatically assumed to hold true for black survivors of incest and child sexual abuse. While there undoubtedly are similarities between black and white survivors as to how incest and child sexual abuse manifests itself, the differences are sufficient to warrant (a) a closer look at social and cultural factors in child sexual abuse; and (b) more direct input by black women survivors into the therapeutic process for dealing with it.

In 1986 two American researchers, Robert Kelly and Merilla Scott, pointed out with respect to sociocultural considerations of CSA that, 'many of us [professionals working in the field] have a tendency to treat all cases of child sexual abuse as though every person came from the same socioeconomic cultural background'. The error, they felt, came as a result of 'concluding that child sexual abuse is a homogeneous problem when . . . it is a problem manifested in diverse ways within our heterogeneous society. Failure to acknowledge this diversity impedes the development of group-specific prevention and treatment programs.'

From the same mould as the homogeneous approach is the tendency to view survivors from a 'colour-blind' perspective. This states that everyone – black or white – should be dealt with in broadly the same manner when it comes to service delivery. The problem with this is that assumptions for working with survivors of sexual abuse are based on a white norm, and take no account, or very little, of the differences, for example in approaches to sexuality of black and white people, and more specifically, of the subtle ways in which racism and sexuality can contribute to misinformed perceptions or preconceptions about black sexuality. (See Chapter 3.)

It is important to say at this point, that though in principle a colour-blind approach is indeed laudable, in practice, faced with a system of finite resources and institutional racism, it leads to black people being disadvantaged generally.

This homogeneous approach is a contributing factor, I feel, to why incest and CSA are not being taken seriously or regarded as problematic by many in black communities. In short, they are ignored, except by those of us whom they touch. In essence, it boils down to restricted, or often, non-existent opportunities for help for black survivors of CSA. None of this, however, comes as a surprise to those of us who are survivors. As a result, many of us *do* feel we have to carry on as if it is all right.

Feminist writer Emily Driver has discussed the inevitable consequences of viewing child sexual abuse as normal in black communities: '[It] not only bolsters society's general racism against all individuals belonging to an ethnic minority group, but also ensures that any abused children within that group are not afforded the same protective and preventive services as other children.'[6] So we have the curious situation that despite all of the information in recent years about the incidence of CSA, relatively speaking, little of it has translated into consideration of CSA in an easily discernible way in black communities.

Devaluation

The effect of all of this is that many black women who have survived incest and CSA often devalue or, perhaps more to the point, underestimate the importance of their experiences as a means of enabling them to reach out to and help others. Either we tend to feel that our experience is unique, and too horrible to share with others; or we suppress it, and consequently overestimate our ability to deal with it all.

> I guess it has to touch your gut for it to affect you. People don't talk about being professional and what that means in terms of relating your own experience to clients. The view among some [women] professionals who are also survivors of CSA is often one of: 'Poor things, I'm helping them, therefore I can't deal with my own abuse.'

> Then one day it hits them. They thought they had come to terms with it. But one day, the self-realisation dawns that they have only been coping on a superficial level. It means you haven't been looking at yourself as a human being as well. They forget that when we step out of the office, we become just like everybody else.

Survivors as professionals

Evidence from survivors who are professionals in the child abuse field is that they run the risk of being taken off cases if they continue to work in a way which exposes their personal experiences, as Liz Kelly points out. That is indeed unfortunate. In preparing this book, I found time and again, that in meeting with survivors, our exchanges frequently became less interview-like and more of a soulful exchange between sister survivors who, above all else, recognised the need that each had, to talk. As black women survivors, in particular, we must get out of the habit of thinking that we cannot share our experiences with each other. There is always the play sister, the good friend, the mother, the therapist. We must begin to challenge the opinion held by some professionals, which dismisses the effectiveness of survivor-led therapy on the basis that objectivity is more important than shared experience in working through the trauma of child sexual abuse. Fortunately, there are those amongst us who have begun the process:

> On the whole I'm not allowed to be a survivor. The part of the profession [social work] I'm in doesn't allow for a lot of things – especially being a survivor.
>
> I take the professional approach and totally forget about my own feelings, in order to work with the person. But there are times when I think that it is important to let the person know that people can survive, and I discuss my own experiences. I find it helps them, and it also helps me. It lets them know that 'it's not just me.' I'm glad when I

can help them feel that they're not the only person this has happened to.

It helps me to talk about it to other women. I feel the more you talk about it, the clearer it gets for yourself. I'm capable of being a client as well as a professional. The degree of credibility you have depends on the client. If I choose to talk about my own experience, it will be after I have got to know them. It will be after a long time, in order to allow me to build up a picture of them and to get an idea of where they're coming from. The way you tell people determines whether your credibility is lost. If you can show you've had a similar experience – it helps. The way I feel is that talking about it as a professional doesn't make you any less of a person.

One black woman, a professional and a survivor who runs discussion groups for women, outlined her thoughts about her work and her survival:

When the six women in the first group disclosed, I didn't. But last week, I began a new group and I disclosed. One woman said it first, and then, I too, disclosed. I thought it would get in the way, but I began to realise that it was disempowering *not* to tell them I understood. I mean, it's empowering. I'm successful at what I do and I feel it's good for these women to see. Incest scars you. But your life doesn't stop and you can use it to be as powerful as you want to be. This is different to thinking though: 'I'm never going to say it.'

Another black woman, also a social worker and a survivor, put it this way:

I work very effectively with children who have been abused and I know other female colleagues who are in a similar position to me [i.e., have also been abused]; but we don't share the fact of our abuse with our managers. They say it blinkers us – that we'll feel, automatically, that the man is guilty. I'm not convinced that's true. My own abuse has given me enormous insight into working with kids; because they'll tell you maybe an inch of what's on their mind, and if they feel you believe them, they'll keep telling you more.

Survival in black and white

Therapy is increasingly becoming recognised as an option by black women who survive incest. So it is important that therapists are aware that the perspective which attaches to black women survivors is different from that experienced by white women. Cultural sensitivity ought to be high on the agenda of therapists who counsel black women. For example, the fact that many black children grow up in single-parent households has a bearing on the development of their sexuality.

Psychotherapist Sonia Francis, whose work with black women survivors includes developing issues concerning their sexuality, notes that in one group of twenty-five women, only five had fathers who were around during their childhoods. Of the five, most had worked out Oedipal (attraction to father) desires quite early on – usually at about the age of three or four. For the vast majority of the others, however, this process was delayed until adolescence.[7]

The taboo against an adolescent girl engaging in sexually flirtatious behaviour with her father or father figures is a strong one in most societies. According to Francis, the notion of black adolescent girls working through their sexuality and their emotions at this later stage becomes explosive. Such expression is greeted with widespread condemnation, particularly in black communities. Girls are labelled promiscuous; are warned against getting pregnant, and are even beaten in an effort to establish control.

The confusion that occurs for some young black women is difficult to express, even harder to understand, and harder still to find a way out of. The case for black women survivors to pool energies and efforts is a strong one. One woman, a survivor and a therapist, put it this way:

> It's a benefit to be both, because you grow up thinking you're the only one it's happening to. We know the intricacies of what people have been through. We do a better job because we have come from the point of surviving.
>
> There is a lot of suspicion about professionals. How can they know the isolation of being a survivor? How do you know they understand what you're telling them? What judgements are they making?
>
> Sometimes people get abused who are in their 20s. In such a situation another survivor would understand that, e.g., no matter how many times you say 'no,' the abuser will still come back. A survivor will not blame another survivor.
>
> A professional might say that if something happens once and you don't want it to happen again, it shouldn't happen again. Survivors know how devastating abuse can be; how nasty it is. Some people are afraid to talk to professionals because they feel they just won't understand. But I've got the experience.

The difficulty for black women who are trying to come to terms with their abuse is that often they are hampered in separating out the black perspective. This has to do with the fact that most therapists are white and inexperienced in dealing with the dimension of race as it impacts on black people. Trained as they are within a white perspective, with a cultural hegemony which automatically assumes a position of dominance, whatever their own politics may be, they may be ill-equipped to deal with the abuse in a way that is comfortable for or comforting to black women.

The added dimension of race can make it more difficult for black women survivors to disclose the abuse to a white counsellor or therapist because of worries about how the information will be interpreted. Fears of negative reactions; of not being believed; of not wanting to have contact with the police; of not wanting to expose oneself to an unsympathetic white professional establishment; of wanting to avoid the stigma of being labelled promiscuous – all of these contribute to black women's silence about their abuse.

> If I were advising another black woman about it, I would encourage her to go to a black counsellor. I thank the Lord I was able to see a black counsellor. White professionals can only go so far. There is that dynamic about colour and race that white professionals have. They have ideas about black women, anyway – that we're whores, that we enticed the men to do it, etc.
>
> It also depends what other abuse, if any, may be going on for black women at the time. I'd like to encourage women to look at what is happening to them, and to talk, because I'm very concerned for black women who don't talk. Talking can either be with a professional or in a group setting.
>
> I always say to black women that I talk to: 'Even if you feel you've failed [because of the incest] the fact that you are here and survived it shows that you have an inner strength.

That inner strength is probably why many in our communities think that we shrug off the abuse and get on with life as if it hadn't happened. Sonia Francis recognises that strength. In her experience, when black women come to therapy they do not come looking for sympathy: 'Black women will come and say: "Let's get down to business and do the work that is necessary for me to overcome this."' There is, says Francis, 'a drive and a will to get to the bottom of it all'.

They approach treatment expecting a more active participation in their own therapy. According to Francis, 'If I make an interpretation to black women, they will usually say something like: "No, that's not right, but this might be the case."' Black women do not come looking to have the answers handed to them, but rather to actively seek a resolution to their confusion and hurt.

Given our history, a history which required our foremothers to survive, often at a terrible cost, this is to be expected. Black women, on the whole, are fighters. We do not give up easily. Our capacity to survive is great. Under slavery, black people had to survive; under colonialism, black people had to survive. We have an innate ability to turn a negative experience into a positive one. This is not the same, however, as saying there are no scars.

The expectation of us – as survivors of incest – that we don't make a fuss or don't dwell on the abuse is unfair and unjust. Its effect on many of us, whether we admit it or even know it, is to create anger and uncertainty. Anger because our survival strategies have been switched around and used against us in a convoluted and misguided attempt to protect an ideal of community, while the reality flounders. Anger because our experiences have been usurped by some in the professional establishment who don't know who we are. Uncertainty because, though we ourselves feel that it is right that we unpack all of this stuff, the active disapproval from our communities which greets our efforts is a severely constraining factor.

CHAPTER 7

Remembering, coping, healing

> The way I feel about incest is that: 'I can survive this.' It's not a positive feeling, more a feeling that you can get beyond it. Every time I go to therapy, I get through it on a deeper level. I even marvel that I can still have everyday life like normal people.

I sometimes wonder how it is that many women who survive childhood sexual abuse manage to do so. We all, if we're lucky, seem to get beyond it with varying degrees of success. But how do we do it?

I met an Afro-German woman two years ago at an international black women's conference held in Germany. A psychologist, she works with black German survivors of incest. Amongst the people she sees, she has identified three groupings: (1) those who don't talk about it; (2) those who talk too much, a factor she regarded as worrying because there was almost too much of an eagerness to divulge their stories, perhaps at the expense of working them through; and (3) those who are aware of it and want to do something positive about exploring its effects on their lives and psyches. The last group was, she said, by far the best group with which to work.

Much the same breakdown can probably be said to exist

amongst all survivors. To varying degrees we remember, or we try to suppress, the abuse; we may even try to ignore it, but it is there nevertheless. Some of us are, indeed, survivors. Others of us are trying to survive, still others are not so fortunate and have decided either not to discuss it or to try to bury it even from themselves; or when the coping mechanisms fail, to bury themselves. What can be said about us, however, is that we all have feelings of vulnerability because of our experience.

Black American writer and lecturer Carolivia Herron, whose recent novel *Thereafter Johnnie*, discusses incest in a black middle-class Washington, DC family, was herself sexually abused as a child of three. She has said that she wakes up every morning to a note pinned to her bed. A note which says: 'Remember not to kill yourself today.'[1]

Perhaps the comment from a black woman at another conference for black women survivors of sexual abuse best sums up how many of us may approach our survival: 'We all want to be empowered to actively deal with our abuse,' she said, 'and we all want to recover from it.'

But what does it mean to be empowered? Does it mean being able to talk about it? Does it mean confronting your abuser? Does it mean being able to touch someone, when you felt you could not get close to another human being? Or does it mean remembering and once you do remember, keeping it together to get through the day, the week, the month, the year? In the words of one survivor:

> Sometimes people don't have memories of being abused, but suddenly, sometimes it just clicks. Sometimes, it's a case of not wanting to remember. But once you do – then come the questions: What triggered the memory? Where has part of you been? How did it happen? Once you face it though, it means you're ready to deal with it.

Another survivor said:

> People avoid pain because their capacity to deal with it is so limited. There are some hurts people can't take and sexual abuse is one of the hardest ones. Suicide was on my agenda throughout my entire adolescence. When I went into therapy I was suicidal; and when I came out I wasn't. I can read the signs now. I'm not ashamed about what happened. I don't feel responsible for what happened, or guilt.

The women whose stories are included in this book have developed many responses to their abuse. They all involve complex coping mechanisms, some of which can show themselves through an unwillingness or inability to trust men, or in a desire to help other victims of sexual abuse:

> I feel I have something to contribute to children who have been sexually abused. My own abuse stops me being judgmental and allows me to be empathetic. That's the survival part. It's saying: 'This is what happened to me and this is how I will redress the balance . . . I work with families in a family centre. It is not just for the children who have been abused. When there has been abuse in a family, I work with the whole family. Most of the families I work with are not black. I want to work with more black families.

In this chapter, I want to put across what can be involved for a black woman in coping with the aftermath (both in the long and the short term) of her sexual abuse. We all approach it in our own unique ways. Though I always remembered my own abuse, I also felt that I couldn't talk about it to others. I knew, however, that I could never run away from it within myself. That way, I could take it out and look at it when I felt I had to, and put it back when I didn't. It was a mechanism which allowed me to focus what happened in my mind, to work through it, to face it;

but in a way that was not destructive to me, that did not overwhelm but allowed me to get on with my life.

In talking with other black women survivors, it was clear that the mechanisms we employ are as varied as the personalities which produce them. Not all of our responses to our abuse can be said to be positive, but they all satisfied the ultimate criterion: that of keeping us sane enough and alive long enough to continue the fight against our respective demons.

Two stories

The following, then, are two stories. Readers, take them and use them if you must, for your own survival. But accept them in the manner in which they are passed on – in the hope that the dialogue which can free us from the silence has begun.

Survivor of incest by father, older male friend of the family and gang-rape

I was eight years old when it started. I grew up in the Caribbean with all boys, and I remember there was a lot of inappropriate touching. I got shipped off to England when I was eight, because my grandmother feared I would be abused.

The first time I remember is at Christmas, being given a present by my dad. There were three younger children in the household and we lived in two cramped rooms. He told me I could have a present if I let him put his hands down my knickers and not tell.

I told my mom, and there was a lot of fussing and shouting. But this was in the context of him kicking her around the front room every week.

After I told my mom, he started knocking me about. He

always hated me and would use any excuse to hit me. There were family conferences about it. I got shipped off to a great-aunt every weekend to stop him hitting me. By the time I was 10 I began to wonder if there was something about me that caused it to happen – because I had been abused in one way or another from four onwards.

My aunt knew why I was there. I stayed at home during the week, and at weekends went to my aunt. My dad worked nights so I didn't see him during the day. I couldn't tell my mum again because I felt she made the choice to stay with my dad, and would say it was my fault, anyway.

When I was 10 we moved to west London. My parents bought a house. Nothing happened for a year. I don't remember his knocking me about, but there was also no physical affection. In a way, I lived like a maid. I was the oldest and had to do all the cooking, cleaning, washing and caring for the other children. I was like a second mother.

I was approaching 12 when something changed. I'd wash my hair and my father offered to dry it; and it was nice, because I didn't get touched in a loving way. But then he started to move his hands down towards my breast and I knew why he had offered to dry my hair. There was no violence, but I knew that if I said anything it would start again.

There was a lot of touching, which led on to penetration of my vagina with his finger – but always when no one was around. At the same time, there was an older male friend of my parents who was sometimes in the house, who used to babysit us. He tried to have sex with me too, and I later learned that he knew what my father was doing. The pay-off from him was sweets.

When I was 12, my grandmother in the Caribbean became ill. My mother had to go to her. It was a terrible time for me because I adored my grandmother. She had raised me until I was eight years old. I remember being weepy one day about this time, and sitting in a park while waiting for clothes to dry in the launderette; and I got gang-raped by four teenage lads.

I never called it rape. They came to me, touching me and taunting me, and I knew what they wanted, so I just laid down and opened my legs. I let it happen. I hadn't had actual sex [intercourse] before. I didn't feel anything – physical pain, yes, but no emotional pain. I remember getting up and hurting and seeing blood on my legs, and searching myself, but I couldn't find where I'd cut myself.

I remember going back to the launderette, as if nothing had happened. My mother was still away and I remember thinking that when she came back I'd have to tell her. I knew before I told her though, that I'd bled from inside. But I thought I'd been hurt, not raped. Ironically, my period started the following month. I now find it difficult to separate my periods from this experience.

I remember the first time my parents' older male friend penetrated me. I remember him trying to have sex with me and asking me who I'd been with, because he managed to penetrate me, after I had been gang-raped. He later said he thought my father had done it.

I remember that period being awful, and feeling suicidal. It was decided that I would go to stay with one of my mother's women friends. When I was staying with her I swallowed a bottle of tablets. I got into bed and got ready to die. I remember waking up and being disappointed. I later learned that the tablets were chalk – a placebo for my mother's friend who was being weaned off valium, following the death of two of her children.

Unknown to me, she told my mother about the suicide attempt. It was in an argument with my mother later that I discovered this. My mother said I could kill myself if I wanted to because she could now afford the coffin.

I had terrible nervous problems. I couldn't read. I did poorly in school. People were concerned.

I disclosed to my aunt about my dad, after she questioned me. She told my mom. There was a big row between the two of them. My dad denied it. My dad's sister said I was lying. I didn't tell about the others. The older male friend of the family was actually having sex with me – my dad was only using his finger inside me. But I didn't tell my mom about that. I didn't think they'd believe me.

I got sent to a psychiatrist and was prescribed valium by our GP. I was 12. The psychiatrist was a dreadful man. *That* was abusive. I wanted to stop going because I felt awful. I hadn't told him about the abuse. I used to sit in silence; so the doctor told my parents there was nothing wrong with me – that I was just missing the Caribbean.

My dad was delighted because I didn't tell the psychiatrist anything. The abuse continued: the older family friend and my dad. The family friend knew about my dad; my dad didn't know about him. My mother pretended not to know.

When I was 13 or 14, I remember being at school and sitting on the loo overdosing on valium. This led to more psychiatric referrals. One woman psychiatrist knew what was going down. After each session, I got questioned by my parents. They were nervous.

When I was 13, my dad started apologising for the abuse. He said it was because I was the image of my mother when he first met her. A lot of it felt displaced. I feel I am the image of my mother. I can remember my father crying when he abused me and saying sorry. He made me bleed as well, because he had long fingernails. I still feel scratched inside. The abuse continued until I was 15.

I survived through the church. I got baptised when I was 12 – after my first suicide attempt. There was a woman in the church who took me under her wing. I loved her. She was like the mother I never had.

When I was 15, my parents took me out of the church. My dad wanted me out because I was becoming effective at avoiding him. My mom, I think, because she wanted me to have boyfriends so that I would leave her husband alone.

When I was 16, I remember coming home from school one day and my mother accusing me of seeing a boy. Dad was no longer abusing me. [He used to make me watch him masturbate though, with a bible in one hand and his penis in the other.] My dad also thought I had boyfriends. He was jealous. He was convinced I was seeing other men – and that that was the reason I didn't want to see him.

There was a big row when I was 18. My dad said I had to go. He said: 'I can't have two women and I'm married to the one upstairs.' My mom cried when I left and everybody felt sorry for her. Everyone blamed me for my mother's crying. But she had told my dad that if he didn't throw me out, she would leave. I couldn't tell anybody. No one would understand.

When I was 21 I went back home for six months. My mom was in hospital. My sister got pregnant at 16. I remember she came after me once because she thought I was after her boyfriend. She accused me in front of her boyfriend of having sex with my father the whole time. All they could think was that I'd done this thing – not that it had been done to me.

My friend, the one who took me in at church, advised me to get help. When I was 22, I got a good counsellor. I was desperate for help. I was suicidal. I felt I was going mad. The neighbours once called the ambulance for me because I couldn't stop crying one night. The sessions with the counsellor were to come to an end, and I was desperate. I think I would have been sectioned if it hadn't been for my friend and the bishop who came to the casualty department to take me home. But I could not tell them why I cried.

Where I'm at today isn't where I'm going to be in five years' time. I'm coherent, but I'm also fragmented. I'm strong, but I can't bear victims. I can't work with victims who want to continue to be victims; who put everything down to being abused. I've no time for it, because I fought so hard to survive. I don't get angry with people who have baggage, but with people who indulge in it.

I can't separate my feelings about men from my abuse. Men don't seem to have developed a language about sex that isn't offensive. I wouldn't tolerate abuse now.

There are also other things for me, e.g. I would never be violent to anyone or hit someone or assault someone. I'm careful about how I am with my partner – I give her lots of space, for example. I could never impose sex.

So, there are positives. You get positives out of negatives.

My parents have now retired to the Caribbean. Two years ago I saw my mother. I had written to her because I wanted to sort things out. She said that if I apologised to her, then she could love me again, like when I was a little girl. All I wanted her to do was to acknowledge that it wasn't my fault. But she didn't. My dad can't be with me without being intimidated. They both live together in misery.

Incest by father and older brother

I come from a big family. There were ten of us. I was the sixth one. There were five boys. We are not a close or affectionate family. People were mainly very sarcastic. There was a lot of put-down in our family.

I'm not sure when it started. After doing therapy, we worked out that I must have been about five. It wasn't brutal, but it was scary. We lived in the North of England, in a big house. I can remember being in my bed. Myself and two other sisters and a brother were in bunk beds. We slept at opposite ends.

I remember my father coming in and my sister saying:

'Go away daddy.' I used to pretend I was asleep and I would shut off. I was 12 or 13 when I started developing breasts. My brother and I used to play fighting games. My brother would pull my top up and touch my breasts.

My dad tried to have intercourse with me when I was 11 or 12. One morning I woke up and I remember his being in the bed. My sister was asleep. The first thing he said was: 'Daddy's come to keep you company.' And I remember thinking: 'That's nice.' Then he said: 'Turn around.' And he tried to push his willie into me.

My body was there, but my mind wasn't. He was not successful and I pushed him off. Afterwards, I went to have a bath, to scrub myself clean. I remember one day resting in my bedroom and he came in. I grabbed my bible and started reading – thinking it would protect me. He had a sneering look on his face, and he said: 'What's the matter with you?' Then he walked out.

When I was in puberty, I felt the world was coming to an end. He kept coming in and touching me. He never penetrated me. He did with my eldest sister though, and with the next sister up from me. He never said anything about it, except for that time when he asked: 'What's the matter?'

I remember he had the same look on his face once, when my sister was sitting crying and writing a letter. My sisters and I never talked about it. My bedroom was right near my mom's, so if she didn't know about it, she must be a very heavy sleeper.

I went to college when I was 16 and it went on for a little while after that, and then it stopped.

Scars

During childhood, I remember I never washed my knickers, I used to hoarde them and hide them. I think it was to do

> with the rape the first time. Periods were another thing that was always traumatic for me.

Once you have been abused it is difficult to know what life would have been like for you if it hadn't happened. Once it has happened, it becomes difficult to regard yourself as other than damaged goods. Quite literally, many of us are physically damaged. One woman described her health problems like this:

> I was 16 or 17 when it ended. I didn't start my period until I was 17½. I had pelvic inflammatory disease for years. My kidney was fucked up – scarred. I had migraines from my teens and before – constant headaches and tummy aches.

The pain and discomfort is not illusory, it is real. And the physical pain is only one part of it. Many women, for example, suffer regularly from panic attacks or severe emotional anxiety every time they think about their abuse or try to recall what happened to them.

The extent of the damage varies and is diverse as the lives we lead. It is important to let it be known what the scarring consists of so that the wounds may be recognised by our families and communities; and possibly, just possibly, moves may be made towards an examination of why they are there in the first place.

On affection

The sexual affection I received from my father provided some of the few memories I have of being physically close to someone in my childhood. The fact that it was an inappropriate closeness, which I nevertheless accepted, leaves one of my most lasting scars. That feeling of culpability has never left me. It is a scar which will take a long time to heal. But it is an acknowledged scar, and that brings a whole new way of dealing with it. Its mystique is removed to some extent, its hold over me; and I can examine it in a personal and political sense.

Though on one level, an intellectual one, I feel that I was not at fault or guilty, on another it seems impossible to move away from the idea (in my innermost thoughts) that I knew better and should have refused. I can imagine some of you thinking now that the guilt should not be mine to carry (and maybe some of you think it should). In a rational sense, maybe it isn't, but as I am discussing scarring I would be less than truthful if I did not admit to the presence of this very deep-rooted scar.

We all carry the scars in different ways – some are deeper than others, some we may not even be aware of until something happens which jars the memory and reawakens the pain. One woman, a survivor, who works with other survivors said of the women who come to her:

> They come and they don't actually say 'I'm supposed to cope,' but you get the feeling they think they are supposed to. They come and they say: 'I've done x, y and z. I shouldn't need to have counselling now for what happened then.' I say to them: 'Yes, it happened a long time ago, but it's having a devastating effect on your life now.' They do start to acknowledge it after a time – when things have gone seriously, critically wrong. There is a repetition of problems. You reach a point where you say: 'I can't go on feeling these feelings.'

Though in one sense we are bound by the similarity of our experiences – the invasion of our bodies by a force more powerful than ourselves – in another we develop many different methods for healing over the gashes in our psyches, and for trying to work out some sense of who we are in the context of the abuse which has irrevocably affected us. One American survivor, Linda H. Hollies, put it this way:

> As I reflect on the experiences and traumas of my childhood, I am amazed and grateful that I have sanity today, but I realize that I have the natural instincts of a survivor. The atmosphere in our home was perhaps similar to a slave labor camp, with father as master and mother as general overseer. There were no loving relationships; we related to my father out of fear and to my mother out of respect. My father used the word love to justify his cruel behaviour – 'it's because I love you that I must whip you.' I recall the one time he asked me if I loved him and I honestly replied, 'No.' He tried to slap the 'hell' out of me. 'Little saved girl, you *must* love your father and respect him as well.' I was an adult, married and pregnant with my first child, when I challenged my mother and heard her say to me, for the very first time, 'I love you.' And they were my primary caregivers, nurturers, protectors from the outside world? From them I was to learn trust and intimacy?[2]

Another survivor said:

> I never went to anyone in authority. It was like I was asleep, and needed to be led. When I went to school I always tried to make friends. I thought I had to try extra hard because I was too dirty. I thought they wouldn't like me. I wasn't allowed to go to Brownies because it was too far and my mother said you never know what's out there in the street [meaning boys]; and I thought to myself, 'I don't have to leave home for that, mom.'
>
> I've been in therapy for three years. The thing about being in a support group is that if you need a hug, you can turn around and it's there. That's important, because it's something that wasn't there when I was a child. Even though my mum and dad may have loved me, I didn't feel it. I felt like one of a number. My only physical contact was with my dad.
>
> Now I give my mum big hugs. But it's a time bomb,

because I think: 'Suppose she knew and I'm hugging her?' My mum said to me not long ago, when we were at a family wedding: 'Give your dad a kiss.' She's done that twice now. Once, when they were going away, my dad pulled me over and gave me a big hug. Afterwards, I totally went to pieces.

I don't want to talk with them about it. My little brother has two girls and one boy. They used to live in the same house with my parents and he [her dad] had access to them. Suppose my niece comes up to me one day and says grandad did something to her?

On loss and trust

What pisses me off is that I lost something I can never regain. I didn't have a childhood. I lost that innocence. I dearly miss that. I wish I'd had a chance to grow up as a child who has not been abused. I'm going through a second childhood now. I could never have children. I'd feel jealous of them – of their innocence. And I'd look at them and think how easy it would be to abuse them. I think I'm afraid that I could abuse them.

Another woman described the sense of loss this way:

At times, when I feel depressed, it gets to me – remembering. I'm strong for 90 per cent of the time, but for that 10 per cent, when things get on top of me, you ask yourself: 'Why me?' I feel that childhood is the most fundamental part of life, and I've been stripped of that. If you've not got the main building blocks, it's harder as an adult to get that back. I hate my dad for that. Now, I go over the top with my kids. My social skills have just started to develop, like making friends or feeling comfortable with people.

As well as the sense of loss we all feel, there are other considerations which are part and parcel of the abuse. Not least of these concern our feelings about men in general, and the relationship of this to our sexuality and ability to feel comfortable with them. I have always been slightly surprised that I didn't end up hating men altogether. Though in truth, I have always felt more of a kinship with women, throughout my life, this has not translated into a rejection of men. I am happily and securely in a relationship with my husband that I would not have dreamed possible.

The feelings of inadequacy surface from time to time, and I deal with them by facing them; by not letting them get in the way of what I want to do in life. Even so, it was a few years into our relationship before I was able to talk about my abuse with my husband. His first reaction was outrage that it had happened to me; his second response was to give support and understanding which has been responsible, in large measure, for showing me another side to the male psyche – a kinder, gentler side – one that does not start from a position of omnipresent sexuality.

The women whose stories appear here have varying degrees of trust, regard and affection for men as a result of their experiences of sexual abuse. Some of them will never be able to trust a man again, because there has been so much damage. The following comments are from survivors who feel that the divide can never be fully crossed again:

> I don't trust men. I can never trust a man again; and if I did, I'd feel I had gone backwards. If I learned to trust that would make me voluntarily vulnerable. Therefore, I have learned to trust with a large degree of caution. I don't think that a woman who has been abused ever really trusts again. I'm in a relationship with a man. We get on fine. But it doesn't mean the fear is not there. I don't lie in bed awake at night. But the fear is that something might trigger a memory from my childhood. How do I know I'm not going to turn over and find a monster next to me?

Another survivor put it this way:

I've never had the feeling of being loved and safe with men. Sex with men is cut off, mechanical. I don't enjoy being close with them. I enjoy having sex with them sometimes, and then I want them to go. It's functional and destructive. My feeling for men is cut off. I have a relationship with their penis. It's like a cash card. On the whole, I have a limited capacity for loving men. They are a different entity to me. I don't get involved with friends' husbands, for example. A lot of them are in awe of me because they attribute many of my attributes to males.

Another woman said of her feelings towards her father:

When I was 25, I realised the effect it started to have on me, I realised I needed therapy. I began to talk about it. And then I felt I needed to get acknowledgement from him – of guilt or remorse. He had no remorse at all. He basically didn't care. He had excuses: It was my mother's fault. I was a very affectionate child. He blamed everybody except himself.

One woman described how she was able finally to end her father's abuse of her:

My friend gave me strength and encouragement. She said: 'Tell him it's not right and that you don't like it; and if he doesn't stop it, you'll tell your mom.' When I first told him, he thought I was messing about. He felt he'd been in control and what was I talking about wanting it to stop. It wasn't straightforward. He still used to come round when my mom was at work. I remember feeling nervous and feeling that I couldn't do it, but my friend helped me.

Another woman spoke of her feelings about her awakening sexuality:

When I was 15 or 16, I started to like guys. But I knew I didn't want anything sexual with them. I liked being chatted up, though. When I was 18 or 19, a group of girlfriends would laugh and joke about the first time they had sex. That's something that I will never be able to talk about.

Beyond incest

We are more, much more, than our experiences of incest and sexual abuse. When I first began, I had hoped that another more appropriate term than survivor, as a description of those of us who have made it 'through the break', would present itself. None has yet emerged. It is important, though, at least to define what it is I mean when I say that we are more than survivors. One woman survivor said: 'I want to thrive, not just survive. I am more than just a survivor. My life cannot simply be summed up as being a survivor.'

In her wonderful and, as ever, insightful essay, 'The Master's Tools Will Never Dismantle the Master's House', Audre Lorde speaks of black women's survival:

> Those of us who stand outside the circle of this society's definition of acceptable women; those of us who have been forged in the crucibles of difference – those of us who are poor, who are lesbians, who are Black, who are older – know that *survival is not an academic skill.* It is learning how to stand alone, unpopular and sometimes reviled, and how to make common cause with those others identified as outside the structures in order to define and seek a world in which we can all flourish. It is learning how to take our differences and make them strengths.[3] (Emphasis added)

For black women who survive incest and other forms of sexual abuse, learning to recognise and utilise our strengths and each other ought to be the first thing on our list of survival mechanisms. In this way lies progress. We learn to create, develop and understand other strategies for survival, ones we may never have considered; ones which complement our nature as black women; and ones we can make our own.

Co-counselling and black spirituality

Patricia Palmer is a therapist who practises her own method of re-evaluation co-counselling. She describes the technique this way:

> Re-evaluation co-counselling helps people get back to their core, to their innate or benign human qualities, recognising or looking at the process of growth and development; looking also at pain, suffering, heartache, and so on.
>
> Re-evaluation co-counselling puts you in touch with the blocks to progress which lie within each individual and which differ according to a person's psychological make-up. Re-evaluation co-counselling is an international organisation which involves people from different cultural backgrounds and social classes.
>
> The majority of co-counselling in the UK involves white people. For a lot of black people, having counselling involves breaking through the barrier of trust. Organisations may be okay, but individuals who practice may not have the best interests of black people at heart. This can be more destructive and damaging for some of the black members.
>
> Black people carry a lot of pain on a deep level. Living in this country as black people, we don't get the chance to look at those hurts over time. Therefore, when we get in an equal opportunity situation, our starting point is different from that of white people. It becomes necessary to free ourselves in order to make changes.
>
> One technique which can help individuals to connect with their true selves is the discharging of the painful emotions they may have internalised, either on a subconscious or conscious basis.
>
> Co-counselling involves changing roles and a talking

through of feelings or thoughts, or it could be about decisions you've made. Each person determines what they want to work on and how they want to divide up the time.

Co-counselling is about the individual knowing what he or she wants. They need to voice what it is they want to do, but not to have judgements made for them. People need to be given time to express themselves and either to affirm or express decisions which have been made, without interference from anyone else.

It's about being present, and feeding back to people. As the process unfolds, bodily changes occur as you break through into areas where you may have been stuck. If co-counselling is effective, you actually feel the changes within the body structure. It can either be shaking, crying, laughing, coughing, sweating, scratching, or whatever.

For black people, it's hard work to get them to admit to carrying grief, sadness, and so on. That's because they say, 'I can cope.' They say that because they've had to cope. But they need to recognise that they have coped by using the grief, or whatever, but that they don't need to continue to use that as a way of resolving things. They can develop new ways of doing things.

In my own work, I look at people's life experiences. I will ask them what it means to be black, for example. It's important for them to realise that they may have had de-humanising experiences that hurt deeply, and that as a consequence, for self-protection, they have established certain mechanisms that inform part of their behaviour.

The converse of that process is that people are encouraged to re-evaluate their lives, and to see how actions which they have taken have led to the present situation. If they are able to get to the root causes and to understand for themselves that they took certain actions that led to certain outcomes, they can change.

The way I work is that they reflect on the past, look at the present, and plan for the future. They receive support for their future plans through the counselling process, and they can also see how their future is tied to their past.

My work is to help people to understand how their life experience has affected them. It is aimed at going through the process of acceptance of the present, then looking at the future – taking what is good from the past. The idea is to find out how to use the painful emotions of the past and the present more constructively. I try to get clients to accept what they feel, and not to be overwhelmed by it, but to find the best ways to deal with what they feel.

With survivors of sexual abuse I try to get them to look at the wider context – at the hurt, pain, rage, guilt. I try to get them to acknowledge what they feel to themselves; that it's okay to feel as they do.

And if it's possible, to get them to go through the experience and look at the reasons why they think they were taken advantage of, recognising that it was wrong. I also encourage people to see that things happen to them that are not their fault, but is more to do with their image/appearance and other people's perceptions, thoughts and feelings. I tell them that rather than suppress their feelings, they should express them and use the experience as part of a teaching/education process.

It's difficult to measure how effective counselling is for people because sexual abuse is very damaging. Some people have moved on and tried to reclaim their power, and to re-structure their lives. They don't forget, but the aim is to free themselves from the hurt and pain of the experiences – not to deny it – but to accept what has happened.

Spirituality

As black women, I feel we have something very special about our lives. We bring something special to this dormant environment. We bring life to this place. A lot of the work around the human psychology/psyche is inappropriate if applied to black people because the concepts have come from people whose concepts are not necessarily to do with human creativity.

For black people, a lot of Eurocentric therapy/counselling is irrelevant. A lot of therapists make blanket assumptions about the theory they've learned. This can result in clients being exploited because they see therapists/counsellors as the experts. Some people go to a counsellor and are not sure why they're going.

Different things work for different people: meditation, reading the Bible, spirituality. Buddhism, for example, facilitates a feeling of being part of and connected to earth and everything in it, and it imparts a need to be respectful for other life on the planet, not just human life. Buddhism is one positive way that people can get the help they need whether they can afford to pay for therapy or not.

The spirituality of the majority of people in this environment is not a living one. It is not based on respect for life, courage, compassion or acceptance of others. It is not based on peace or friendship. Therefore disconnection from the environment and people is greater. A lot of the pain that black people experience has to do with their disconnection from their own spirituality. Everything to do with black people's spirituality has been denied and we have been taught not to feel it. We have been taught to despise it. So invariably, we do not understand it or own it.

At the end of the day, the root cause of our suffering is our disconnectedness from our human selves. One of the major hurts we have is the suppression of that spirituality, which wants to be alive, free, happy and contented.

Rebirthing

Zhana is a personal growth consultant, who uses the rebirthing technique, among others, to help women arrive at the strategies they need. Rebirthing, she says, allows our subconscious thoughts to come to the surface. It is conscious, connected breathing, inhaling and exhaling, to reach a state where you are in touch more completely with yourself and with whatever is going on in your life. Although mainly used by white women and men, it is a technique which some black women therapists, like Zhana, also find effective. That is because rebirthing helps to create the safe spaces that we all need – space to be vulnerable, space to ask for support, and space to heal. This ability to connect with ourselves in this way is especially important for black women, given our stereotypical image of harshness and brashness, images that frequently obscure even our own views of self, and that get in the way of our asking for help;

or, once we do, they prevent us from working out what is appropriate to our needs. One black woman who has done rebirthing described her experience this way:

> I have been doing affirmation which says it's alright to be slim. The idea of slimness has been the cause of a lot of pain for me. I had this idea that it wasn't safe to be slim because to be small was to be vulnerable; also that my body was not safe, because this female body was making this poor man feel out of control. But I've been doing spontaneous rebirthing to help me.

Anger as a strategy

I was part of a one-day workshop in a south London women's centre a couple of years ago. It was a session which I had gone to as part of my research for this book. I had not intended to become a participant, but had attended instead as a recorder and an observer. I soon found myself drawn into the session, despite my attempts at objectivity.

What came across to me most clearly, and which I understood as well as those women in that session, were the feelings of repressed and confused anger, as well as feelings of betrayal that the women felt as a consequence of their abuse. All of us had been sexually abused as children. All, with the exception of myself, were in various stages of counselling for it. All were still trying to come to terms with the abuse many years later. Some were trying to remember, sifting through fleeting and hazy images; others were slowly beginning to retrieve it from the far reaches. Still others were unsure of the next step, but determined to take it.

The lasting image I have of that session is of the anger that permeated it; an anger which served to keep some of the women focused and thus empowered to deal with the realities and the consequences of their abuse. An anger which was pure and clean; straightforward and honest; undaunted and unswerving. An anger which said this should not have happened to me, but since it has, I'm going to hold on to my anger in order to hold on to myself.

Audre Lorde has written that, as black women, we often misuse our anger:

> We have wasted our angers too often, buried them, called them someone else's, cast them wildly into oceans of racism and sexism from which no vibration resounded, hurled them into each other's teeth and then ducked to avoid the impact. But by and large, we avoid open expression of them, or cordon them off in a rigid and unapproachable politeness. The rage that feels illicit or unjustified is kept secret, unnamed, and preserved forever . . . And certainly, there are enough occasions in all our lives where we can use our anger righteously, enough for many lifetimes.[4]

My argument here is that there is no more righteous use of our anger than in directing it against those who have abused us; those who would abuse us and our children; or those who expect us to remain silent about the abuse. That is what the women in that workshop recognised; that is what is important for us all, as survivors, also to recognise. In this way we can work towards getting rid of the tendency to 'medicalise' the healing process.

Getting in touch with our feelings to the extent that we focus our anger – channel it to help us reclaim who we are – should be of primary importance to us all. We owe it to ourselves to work towards healing ourselves in a way which is beneficial and consistent and which involves the establishment of a positive ethos in how we live our lives as black women and as black people. That, I feel, is a productive use of anger. As a child, I can remember my grandmother saying, 'The truth will set you free.' For incest survivors, I feel it is our anger which will set us free.

That anger can, however, take many different forms,

not all of them beneficial or positive: for example the self-mutilations many women carry out on themselves, or the eating disorders that can develop because they are not in touch with the abuse or their feelings – angry or otherwise – about it. According to one black therapist who works with both black and white survivors of child sexual abuse, 'Black women don't seek therapy.' This may be due, in part, to a lack of understanding about what it is or what it involves; it may be due to lack of money (therapy is, after all, expensive), or it may be a belief that there is a stigma attached to asking for therapeutic help.

The Lambeth Women and Children's Health Project

Help is available. One place where black women in London who have been sexually abused can go for help is the Lambeth Women and Children's Health Project, based in Brixton. The project counsels women who have been sexually abused as children, works with mothers of sexually abused children; and carries out child protection training.

The project's co-ordinator is Pat Agana. Her experience in working with survivors is that they have learned, as children, to regard sex as affection. It is, she says, 'the Lolita concept'. A child who has been sexually abused will have been taught to behave in a certain way in order to get the love and affection they want. A girl child will have learned to go and sit on daddy's lap or to bare her shoulders or to raise her dress in front of daddy. She may then be labelled precocious or provocative, and said to want sex. It must be borne in mind, says Pat Agana, that a child is not born with her legs open, bent on attracting men.

The point to remember, she says, is that 'the child has been *taught* to accept sexual abuse as love and affection'. The message is put across that sexual abuse is loving. It reminds me a bit of something called the hostage syndrome.

It was discovered that hostages, like those taken in aeroplane hijackings in the Middle East, do, after a time, begin to identify with their captors: to the point that when they are released they express sympathies with them, despite the undoubted ordeal of their captivity. In a similar way, survivors of child sexual abuse also have to come to terms with these feelings – feelings of attachment; of love; of not wanting to betray the perpetrator.

'Let's get down to what is really happening,' said Pat Agana, 'which is that every child is born willing to interact with his or her environment; willing to trust; willing to learn. Our lives are based on the experiences we have, and it's that learning which conditions our responses, which determines what becomes normal for us.'

What makes a woman come to counselling?

Some women come to the project, says Pat Agana, because

> they reach a point where they can't take any more. The first thing I tell them is, 'Whatever you did in your life that kept you in control was good, because it meant that you stayed alive.' But when they come here, it's because whatever that thing was that held it together for them, doesn't work any more. Everything comes crashing down. They may go for a big job and feel they're not worthy of getting it. At the same time, there is an awareness from within that it is to do with being sexually abused as a child.

The project stipulates that women who come for help must take the active step to do so. The woman must make the phone call. When she comes to the project, it is with an explicit awareness that she is coming to work on her feelings and attitudes about her sexual abuse. The project does not treat sexual abuse as an illness. Nor does it foster a dependency on therapy, which can lead some women to feel unable to make a decision without first consulting their therapist.

An attempt is also made to acknowledge the nature of the relationship between the therapist and the woman. According to Agana:

> We are aware that power is an integral part of it, and however good a counsellor may be, it's a test for us too. As therapists, we need to acknowledge that power relationship, because it is a reality of people's interaction with each other. We don't necessarily need to compensate for it, but we do need to be aware of it.

Counselling is for a total of six one-hour sessions. The duration is the same for the woman who comes to therapy because she is self-mutilating as for the woman who may not even be aware of or have been able to remember her abuse. The idea is to do a concentrated piece of work with a woman, with the aim of allowing her to get beyond her current crisis and back in control of her life. 'Sex abuse is not the person,' said Agana. 'It is an issue in their lives now and one which they need to get control over now.'

The Lambeth project also aims to pass on skills to women to enable them to come to the realisation that what a counsellor can do for them, they can do for themselves. Part of the thinking in this regard is to prevent the therapist from becoming too enmeshed in the women's lives. After many years' work in the field of child sexual abuse, Agana has seen many therapists 'disappear down the plughole, because they try to save the world. This way, I can help them to work out what can be done and not get destroyed in the process.'

Step by step

A six-hour programme has been developed by the Lambeth Women and Children's Health Project. The following is an outline of how it works, on a week-by-week basis. It is informed by Pat Agana's years of working in the London Rape Crisis Centre, where, she says, she began to realise that the women who used the centre (mainly white) were bound together only by their experience of sexual abuse, and nothing else: 'When people came together, they denied their histories, so what they were presenting was only half a self.' The project's programme has set out to ameliorate this situation with an approach which seeks to inform and include the whole self. Agana describes the programme:

First week: Preliminaries. We start by finding out what women want when they come; why they come; what they hope to achieve. We place a great emphasis on who the women are and what their social and emotional experiences are. We start from the position that what a woman needs is what she *knows* she needs, *not* what a counsellor or therapist tells her she needs.

We start with women coming to talk about where they are now. That 'now' may be no job; or 'my lover/husband is tired of hearing me talk about it and I need to see someone about this.' All of the women who come to us self-refer. We don't take referrals from agencies, GPs, etc. If a woman comes it's because that's what she wants to do now. You can't make a phone call on behalf of someone else.

One of the first things we tell them is to get two notebooks – one for dreams and one for the different exercises that we do. We ask them to take a half-hour each day, during the first week, to think about the abuse. About every single thing to do with it. The point about this is that *they* are choosing the time. The thing about sexual abuse is that it can take you over – a sound, a smell, seeing the person, can trigger the whole thing, and bring on panic attacks, for example.

But when a woman chooses a time to think about it, it gives her a time when she can face it head-on. It affects women in various ways – one woman used to smash plates;

one woman used to self-mutilate, then she ended up by smoking. It's not good to smoke, true enough, but for her it was good, because it meant it was a way of enabling her to control her feelings about the abuse.

It's a simple, but intensive way of recalling the abuse; and bit by bit it comes back, and soon they're able to get the whole picture.

We encourage women to take notes during the half-hour, about their feelings and thoughts. At the end of the first week, we discuss what they have written and been through emotionally. The most important thing, however, is that no matter what method is used to deal with the abuse, it should involve separating emotions about the abuse from the abusive act itself.

When a woman needs help, often it's the emotions which are coming back. The purpose of these half-hour sessions is to put the emotions in perspective; for example, the anger gets put in the right place, and doesn't leap out at you every time, for example, you see an old, bald man who might remind you of your abuser.

Second week: In this week, the woman talks about her different feelings, even realises some of her feelings. For example, one woman didn't like to lie on her back, even in intimate relations, and she didn't know why. We also start to look at other people in the woman's life – for example, other relations. We look at positive and negative things.

Third week: Next we do a singular piece of work around a particular individual. Often women want to know at this point, 'Where was my mother? She must have known.' This is a particularly important point, because whether the mother did or did not know, there will always be something in the back of a child's head which will hold the mother responsible.

It's important to say that this is different from the dysfunction theory, which *starts* by blaming the mother. According to this view, the mother should be all-seeing, all-knowing, all-caring. What we try to make clear is *not* that the mother is responsible, but that as *part* of the process, a child will blame the mother.

It's a chicken and egg process. Does it start with the mother? It certainly doesn't start with the newborn baby girl, who is receptive to learning. But often society begins with the idea of blaming the mother. I draw a parallel with the person that first split the atom; I don't think that that person planned on Hiroshima.

Fourth week: We begin the fourth week with a question: If all was well with the world, where would you want to be a year from now? Women are now prepared to think about these things, and are encouraged to free-think. For example, they are encouraged to think about who they were before the abuse took place. They go right back to the stage where they were playing with dolls, or whatever, and all kinds of things come from this. Sometimes women say: 'I used to paint', or 'I used to play guitar', or maybe that they'd always felt a desire to lead an organisation, or even to get a car.

By this fourth week we are forward-looking. In the first week, we ask women if they have told anyone about their abuse. The response is usually a horrified no. By the fourth week, they have told someone. That someone could be the woman who is a weekly swim companion or it might be her mother.

Fifth week: We get down to the business of sorting out all of the things that a woman wants to accomplish over the next 12 months. That could be a job or career change, or a health issue. The way I like to think about it is that child sexual abuse is another bit of the jigsaw that affects a woman's health, or state of well-being. We encourage women, if they need to, to make use of the other services we offer. We feel it's a good thing, because we are a health programme.

I am here to help them correct the mis-information they have been given about who they are and what they are. I point out to them that their abuser passed through their lives, and did what they did, yes. But their lives are bigger than the abuse that happened to them.

Sixth week: We go back over the journals, dreams and diaries, looking at them in a new context. It is now contained. Life has moved on. There is also an intangible change, of coming out of the depression. The sexual abuse remains a reality, and there will be times when remembering it gets out of control again. What's different is that the woman now knows how to deal with it.

I feel this approach is useful because it respects cultures, norms and social issues. A Latin American woman can come and go through the process, and go back to her lifestyle in the same way that a black or white woman from Britain can. It's about getting women to realise that their lives are bigger than to be limited by this experience of sexual abuse. Some women get stuck and feel that they can't do anything other than what they are doing, even though they are unhappy.

We say to women – If you can't love yourself, you can't love anyone else. There is a thread of self that if damaged or attacked, or not allowed to develop, leaves people thinking that they're not worth anything. But I believe that each and every woman has a right to occupy an uninvaded space on this earth, and to engage in a life emanating from herself, rather than in reaction to forces trying to deny her spirit.

Towards healing the communal wounds

> The number one issue for most of our sisters is violence – battering, sexual abuse. Same thing for their daughters, whether they are twelve or four. We have to look at how violence is used, how violence and sexism go hand in hand, and how it affects the sexual response of females. We have to stop it, because violence is the training ground for us.
>
> When you talk to young people about being pregnant, you find out a lot of things. Number one is that most of these girls did not get pregnant by teenage boys; most of them got pregnant by their mother's boyfriends or their brothers or their daddies. We've been sitting on that. We can't just tell our daughters, 'just say no.' What do they do about all those feelings running around their bodies? And we need to talk to our brothers. We need to tell them, the incest makes us crazy. It's something that stays on our minds all the time. We need the men to know that. And they need to know that when they hurt us, they hurt themselves. Because we are their mothers, their sisters, their wives; we are their allies on this planet. They can't just damage one part of it without damaging themselves. We need men to stop giving consent, by their silence, to rape, to sexual abuse, to violence.[5]

When I started thinking seriously about writing this book, I thought first and foremost that it should be primarily for black women. And so it is. But it would be less than complete if it did not also speak to black men. It would be remiss of me not to urge them to acknowledge their part in causing the pain and hurt which continues, unabated, in the lives of black women who have been sexually abused. It is pain and hurt which has a stranglehold on our communities because of their inability or unwillingness to participate in a dialogue with us or to assume responsibility for their actions, and equally, their inaction.

It is not pleasant to think about. It is painful and embarrassing to talk about. It is a blight on our communities.

Nevertheless, it exists. And failure to acknowledge the abuse, and its effect on black women who survive it, must be looked at squarely and with no illusions about its occurrence.

It is important to try to understand why it is men who primarily commit sexual abuse. As I said earlier, part of the reason is to be found in macho male perceptions of women's sexuality, especially black women's sexuality. Part of it lies in a male socialisation which fails to instil compassion and instead promotes sexual conquest as a desirable act; part of it lies in the taken-for-granted sexism that characterises our everyday lives.

> I finally told somebody four years ago [said a 34-year old survivor]. This man, my so-called 'uncle', raped another girl of 17. Once everybody said it was him, that did it. I felt safe to tell somebody. I told my stepfather. That was the release for me. I realised then it wasn't my fault, but that this is how this man is. The rest came out in therapy. My mother died 12 years ago. When I disclosed my stepfather was very angry. I felt he was feeling responsible for the act of this man. He was so angry. He said: 'Men like that make other men look bad.' But I feel it has to come out. When I talked to my brother about it, he felt completely threatened. He had a similar reaction to my stepfather and he felt the need to remove it from himself. They didn't want to understand it because they were worried that they would be tarred with the same brush.

The fears that black people have about all black men being 'tarred with the same brush' are real ones. Earlier I discussed the sexual stereotyping which impedes a frank discussion of sex and sexuality in our communities. However, given the reality that sexual abuse exists in our communities, and is perpetuated primarily against female children – let us not forget the harm that results from it. I find that, as a survivor of incest, I have no room for the argument that says do nothing because to do anything will reflect badly on us as a community. I wonder if the same sentiment would hold if the numbers were reversed and it was countless numbers of little black *boys* who were being seduced by their fathers (or their mothers, even). I hasten to add that there is little doubt that boys are victimised by sexual abuse, but I would argue that it is not nearly to the same extent, and if it were, the attitudes surrounding it would not be so casual, nor the silence so complete.

Where does all this leave us as black people? Again, I would turn to Finkelhor, who argues that there are 'clear implications about social changes that could help to eliminate sexual abuse':

> First, that men might benefit from the opportunity to practice affection and dependency in relationships that did not involve sex, such as male-to-male friendships and nurturant interaction with children. Second, that the accomplishment of heterosexual sex might be de-emphasized as the ultimate criterion of male adequacy. Third, that men might learn to enjoy sexual relationships based on equality.[6]

These criteria should not be applied any less stringently because the perpetrator of the incest is a black man. Nowhere is it written (or if it is, it shouldn't be) that black men should be let off the hook, and that they are unaccountable because of the extenuating circumstances of race, poverty and economic disadvantage. Little black girls are entitled to receive, and to feel safe in receiving, affection and nurturing from their fathers, uncles, male friends of the family, grandfathers, etc. without the inappropriate boundary-crossing which incest and other forms of child sexual abuse entails.

My hope is that black people will come away with this message first and foremost, because it is only through the fundamental acceptance of this tenet that black communities – survivors and perpetrators alike – can free ourselves of this yoke of silence which threatens to engulf, and which may eventually destroy us, if we fail to confront it honestly and work to rid our communities of it.

EPILOGUE

Many people have asked if I have found writing this book a cathartic experience. If by that is meant the dictionary definition of the word – as a purgative or cleansing process – the answer must be yes *and* no.

Yes, it has been a catharsis in that I feel I have finally faced the mechanics of my experience of incest – what happened, why I think it happened, and how I deal with it on an intellectual level. In the thirty-odd years since it happened, I feel I have been successful in dealing with it on that basis. The skeletons have been laid bare and there are no more dark corners.

On another level I hope, and really feel, that this book will be useful to the many black women who have had experiences of incest and other forms of sexual abuse. It's never easy to acknowledge. In talking with many women, however, both those who are survivors and those who aren't, I sense a groundswell of support for putting the issue of child sexual abuse on the table, as far as black people are concerned. I feel privileged to be part of that process, and I write very much from the position that what is included in this book is there to be used. My aim is that people will take from it what they need – on a personal or a political level.

Writing the book has been a very hard process – mentally, physically and emotionally. Mentally remembering and physically structuring, restructuring and contextualising the information into a usable and useful format has been a huge task. In addition, the sheer willpower it has taken to keep going when I have, at times, doubted whether I could see the project through to its conclusion has demanded clarity and emotional resolve.

The support of all those women and others who kept reminding me that it was a worthwhile thing to do; that I was right to want to do it; and that there were many black women out there who needed such a book has sustained me throughout. It has been invaluable to me. Not only has it enabled me to find the words that I know needed to be said, but it has meant that the catharsis set in motion with the first germ of an idea about how to structure the book has been superseded by the very real sense of sisterhood and love I have found.

But no, I am not cleansed of the memory of the incest. I will never forget it. It is not possible for me to do so, especially when there are so many reminders that abuse clearly goes on. I feel, however, that I have reached a point where the incest no longer defines me as a person. I have very much moved beyond it in that sense. Such a step is a giant one to take in the road to recovery.

And so, the catharsis continues. Not an end, but a beginning, for myself, and for all those out there, who are waiting to break through their silences. The path to survival and wholeness is open.

RESOURCES

R. Christine Angell, MFCC (Marriage, Family and Child Counselor) specializes in women's issues, recovery issues, spirituality, co-dependency and ACA's, inner child work, and survivors of abuse.
445 Bellevue Avenue, Suite 103
Oakland, CA 94610
(510) 835-9805

Lorene Garrett-Browder, LCSW is an African-American therapist working with black women survivors and those from other ethnic groups.
Alliance Community Counseling Center
1014 Lincoln Avenue
San Jose, CA 95125
(408) 293-4489

Le Ann Tisdale-Perez, LMFCC is an African-American therapist working with black women survivors and those from other ethnic groups.
1777 Hamilton Avenue #212
San Jose, CA 95125-5410
(408) 266-5800

The Healing Woman is a monthly newsletter for women survivors of childhood sexual abuse.
P.O. Box 3038
Moss Beach, CA 94038
(415) 728-0339

Survivors & Friends is a newsletter for incest survivors and their families.
P.O. Box 54
Redmond, WA 98073
(206) 821-8523

Feminist Women's Health Center works with black women, referrals for self-help groups.
580 14th Street NW
Atlanta, GA 30318
(404) 875-7115

The Norma J. Morris Center for Healing from Child Abuse (formerly Adult Survivors of Incest Foundation, Inc.) offers information on meetings and self-help groups.
2306 Taraval Street, Suite 102
San Francisco, CA 94116-2252

National Black Women's Health Project is a self-help and health advocacy organization.
1237 R.D. Abernathy Blvd., SW
Atlanta, GA 30310
(404) 758-9590

Incest Resources offers literature, tapes, newsletters. Send self-addressed business envelope with 58 cents postage; ask for IR fliers.
46 Pleasant Street
Cambridge, MA 02139

Incest Survivors Anonymous
P.O. Box 17245
Long Beach, CA 90807-7245

Incest Survivors Information Exchange
P.O. Box 3399
New Haven, CT 06515

Survivors of Incest Anonymous offers 12-step literature and information about support groups. For group directory, send self-addressed business envelope, 58 cents postage. Newcomer packet $5 (free if you can't afford it.)
P.O. Box 21817
Baltimore, MD 21222

VOICES (Victims of Incest Can Emerge Survivors) in Action is a national network for incest survivors, and offers literature, referrals, newsletters and conferences.
P.O. Box 148309
Chicago, IL 60614
1-800-786-4238

NOTES

Chapter 1
Myths, realities and matriarchy

1 M. Bogle, Speech at Conference on, 'Child Sexual Abuse: Towards a Feminist Professional Practice', 6–8 April 1987, Polytechnic of North London.
2 L.H. Pierce and R.L. Pierce, 'Race as a Factor in the Sexual Abuse of Children', in *Social Work Research Abstracts*, National Association of Social Workers, New York 1984.
3 D. Russell et al., 'The Long-Term Effects of Incestuous Abuse. A Comparison of Afro-American & White American Victims', in G.E. Wyatt and G.J. Powell (eds), *The Lasting Effects of Child Sexual Abuse*, Sage Publications, London, 1988.
4 K. Jackson, 'A Step towards Multiculturalism', Report on panel discussion at New York Women Against Rape Fifth Annual Conference, New York 1984.
5 Kris, in *Gossip*, 1986, pp.81–82, 88.
6 L. Hollies, 'A Daughter Survives Incest: A Retrospective Analysis, *Sage*, 4(2), Fall 1987.
7 Khadj Rouf in *Bandung File: Tell It Like It Is*, 28 November 1989.
8 Signs are that this attitude is changing, amid an increasing awareness among, for example, women in Jamaica who have begun work around issues of incest and child sexual abuse in that country. These comments were made at a workshop on black women and sexual abuse, 1991 Cross-Cultural Black Women's Studies Institute, July/August, 1991, Frankfurt, Germany.
9 Sonia Sanchez in B. Lanker, 'I Dream A World. Portraits of Black Women who Changed America', Stewart, Tabori and Chang, New York, 1989.
10 G.E. Wyatt, 'The Sexual Abuse of Afro-American and White American Women in Childhood', *Child Abuse & Neglect*, 9, 1985, pp.507–519.
11 D. Russell, *The Secret Trauma. Incest in the Lives of Girls and Women*, Basic Books, New York, 1986.

12 L. Kelly, et al., *An Exploratory Study of the Prevalence of Sexual Abuse in a Sample of 16–21 Year Olds*, Child Abuse Studies Unit, Polytechnic of North London, 1991.
13 C. Poston and K. Lison, *Reclaiming Our Lives. Hope for Adult Survivors of Incest*, Little Brown, Boston 1989.
14 S. Forward and C. Buck, *Betrayal of Innocence. Incest and its Devastation*, Penguin Books, Harmondsworth, 1978.
15 J. Goodwin, 'Obstacles to Policymaking about Incest – Some Cautionary Tales', in G.E. Wyatt and G.J. Powell (eds), *The Lasting Effects of Child Sexual Abuse*, Sage Publications, London, 1988, p.25.
16 B. Gilroy, Personal interview, August, 1991, Frankfurt, Germany.
17 B. Richie-Bush, 'Facing Contradictions: Challenge for Black Feminists', *Aegis*, 37, 1983.
18 Goodwin, op. cit, p.29.
19 Richie-Bush, p.16.
20 In Michele Wallace, *Black Macho & the Myths of the Superwoman*, John Calder, London, 1979.

Chapter 2

Incest in the work of black women writers

1 M. Angelou, *I Know Why the Caged Bird Sings*, Virago, London, 1984.
2 M. Angelou, in C. Tate ed., *Black Women Writers at Work*, Continuum, New York, 1983.
3 P. Parker, 'Shoes', and comments in E. Bass et al. (eds), *I Never Told Anyone: Writings by Women Survivors of Child Sexual Abuse*, Perennial Library, New York, 1983.
4 A. Walker, *The Color Purple*, Women's Press, London, 1983.
5 M. H. Washington, *Black-Eyed Susans: Classic Stories by and about Black Women*, Anchor Books, New York, 1975.
6 Brixton Black Women's Group, *Speak Out*, 5 (December), 1983.
7 Washington, *Black-Eyed Susans*, p.xiii.
8 M. Wallace, *Black Macho & the Myth of the Superwoman*, John Calder, London, 1979, p.107.
9 Z.N. Hurston, *Their Eyes Were Watching God*, Virago, London, 1986, quoted in M.H. Washington, op.cit., p.xi.
10 S. Boyce, Mr. Friend of a Family.
11 S. Francis, Personal Interview, 2 May, 1991.

12 B. Emecheta, *Gwendolen*, Flamingo, London, 1990.
13 J. Riley, *The Unbelonging*, Women's Press, London, 1985.
14 Washington, *Black-Eyed Susans*, p.xxxi.
15 O.P. Adisa, *Bake-Face and other Guava Stories*, Flamingo, London, 1989, p.11.

Chapter 3

Black women, sex and sexuality

1 A. Rich, 'Husband-Right and Father-Right', in *On Lies, Secrets and Silence: Selected Prose 1966–1978*, Virago, London, 1977.
2 B. Holiday, 'Lady Sings the Blues', in E. Bass et al. (eds), *I Never Told Anyone: Writings by Women Survivors of Child Sexual Abuse*, Perennial Library, New York, 1983, pp.176–7.
3 In D. Russell, *The Secret Trauma: Incest in the Lives of Girls and Women*, Basic Books, New York, 1986, p.193.
4 *The Guardian*, 18 February 1992.
5 A. Lorde, 'Sexism: An American Disease in Blackface', in *Sister Outsider*, Crossing Press, Trumansburg, N.Y, 1984.
6 Y. Badoe (dir.), *I Want Your Sex*, Channel 4 [UK], 3 November 1991.
7 D. Dabydeen, on *I Want Your Sex*.
8 C. Mercer, on *I Want Your Sex*.
9 F. Fanon, *Black Skin, White Masks*, Grove Press, New York, 1967.
10 B. Gilroy, Personal interview, August, 1991, Frankfurt Germany.
11 E. Cleaver, *Soul on Ice*, Dell, New York, 1968.
12 A. Lorde, *Sister Outsider*, p.61.
13 A. Walker, 'Coming Apart', in *You Can't Keep A Good Woman Down*, Women's Press, London, 1982.
14 M. Wallace, in *I Want Your Sex*, op. cit.
15 D. Russell et al., 'The Long-term Effects of Incestuous Abuse: A Comparison of Afro-American and White American Victims', in G.E. Wyatt and G.J. Powell (eds), *The Lasting Effects of Child Sexual Abuse*, Sage, London, 1988.
16 P. Agana, 'Training for Life' (transcript of a speech), in M. Sulter (ed.), *Passion: Discourses on Blackwomen's Creativity*, Urban Fox Press, Hebden Bridge West Yorkshire, 1990, pp.146–7.
17 Lorde, *Sister Outsider*, pp.47–48.

18 M. MacLeod and E. Saraga (eds), *Child Sexual Abuse: Towards a Feminist Professional Practice*, proceedings of conference, 6–8 April 1987, Polytechnic of North London.
19 Lorde, *Sister Outsider* pp.47–49.
20 Agana, 'Training for Life' (transcript of a speech), in M. Sulter (ed.) *Passion: Discourses on Blackwomen's Creativity*, op. cit.
21 T. Morrison, *Ebony*, July, 1988.

Chapter 4

Love, comfort and abuse

1 S. Francis, Personal interview, 2 May 1991.
2 S. Nelson, *Incest, Fact and Myth*, Stramullion Co-operative, Edinburgh 1987.
3 F. Rush, *The Best Kept Secret: Sexual Abuse of Children*, McGraw-Hill, New York, 1980.
4 P. Agana, Personal interview, 4 February 1992.
5 S. Francis, Personal interview, 2 May 1991.
6 In D. Russell, *The Secret Trauma: Incest in the Lives of Girls and Women*, Basic Books, New York 1986, pp.193–4.
7 Agana, Personal interview, 4 February 1992.
8 'Statistics of a Taboo', *New Statesman & Society*, 1 July 1988.
9 L.H. Hollies, 'A Daughter Survives Incest', *Sage*, 4 (2), Fall 1987.
10 L. Kelly et al., *An Exploratory Study of the Prevalence of Sexual Abuse in a Sample of 16–21-Year-Olds*, Child Abuse Studies Unit, Polytechnic of North London, 1991.
11 'When a Woman Says No', *Spare Rib*, May 1990.
12 *Essence* magazine, March 1992.

Chapter 5

Towards a black feminist understanding of child sexual abuse

1 M. Rodriguez-Alvarado, of the Commission for the Improvement of Women's Rights, Puerto Rico, 'Rape and Virginity among Puerto Rican Women', *Aegis*, March/April 1979.
2 E. Saraga and M. MacLeod, *Child Sexual Abuse: Towards a Feminist Professional Practice*, proceedings of conference, 6–8 April 1987, Polytechnic of North London.
3 Ibid.
4 M. Wallace, *Black Macho & the Myth of the Superwoman*, John Calder, London, 1979.

5 A. Lorde, *Sister Outsider*, p.74.
6 P. Agana, 'Training for Life', in M. Sulter (ed.), *Passion: Discourses on Blackwomen's Creativity*, Urban Fox Press, Hebden Bridge, W. Yorkshire, 1990.
7 A. Dworkin, *Intercourse*, Secker & Warburg, London, 1987.
8 A. Davis, *Women, Race and Class*, Women's Press, London, 1982.
9 Wallace, *Black Macho*, pp.106–7.
10 b. hooks, *Yearning, Race, Gender and Cultural Politics*, Turnaround Books, London, 1991, p.214.
11 A. Walker, *Meridian*, Women's Press, London, 1982.
12 S. Francis, Personal interview, 2 May 1991
13 K. Jackson of New York Women Against Rape, in *Aegis*, 37, 1983.
14 M. Bogle, speech at Polytechnic of North London, April 1987.
15 M. MacLeod and E. Saraga, 'Child Sexual Abuse: A Feminist Approach', *Spare Rib*, August 1987.
16 P.H. Collins, 'The Meaning of Motherhood in Black Culture and Black Mother/Daughter Relationships', *Sage*, 4 (2), Fall 1987.
17 M. Mtezuka, 'Towards a Better Understanding of Child Sexual Abuse among Asian Communities', *Practice*, Autumn/Winter 1989–90.
18 S. Nelson, *Incest: Fact and Myth*, Stramullion Co-operative, Edinburgh, 1987.
19 See D. Russell, *The Secret Trauma: Incest in the Lives of Girls and Women*, Basic Books, New York, 1986.
20 D. Russell et al., 'The Long-term Effects of Incestuous Abuse. A Comparison of Afro-American and White American Victims', in G.E. Wyatt and G.J. Powell (eds), *The Lasting Effects of Child Sexual Abuse*, Sage, London, 1988.
21 J. Perez, 'A Step towards Multiculturalism', panel discussion, Women Against Rape Fifth Annual Conference, New York, 1984.
22 K. Farrell, 'The London Rape Crisis Centre and Black and Ethnic Minority Women', Report, March, 1990.
23 M. Elliott, speech at Kidscape's First National Conference on Female Abusers, London March 1992.
24 R. Mathews, J.K. Matthews and K. Speltz, *Female Sexual Offenders: An Exploratory Study*, Safer Society Press, Vermont, 1989.

25 L. Kelly, 'Unspeakable Acts', *Trouble and Strife*, 21, Summer 1991.
26 NSPCC, *Child Abuse Trends in England and Wales 1983–1987*, NSPCC, July, 1989, London.
27 NCH/DoH, *The Report of the Committee of Enquiry into Children Who Sexually Abuse Other Children*, NCH, London April 1992.
28 b. hooks, *Talking Back: Thinking Feminist – Thinking Black*, Sheba, London, 1989.
29 D. Finkelhor, *Child Sexual Abuse New Theory and Research*, The Free Press, New York, 1984. pp.11–12.
30 D. Finkelhor, ibid. p.6.
31 D. Finkelhor, ibid.

Chapter 6

Success, survival and the professional incest industry

1 L. Hollies, 'A Daughter Survives Incest', *Sage*, 4 (2), Fall 1987.
2 *The Lancet*, 16 April 1988.
3 L. Kelly, Personal interview, 10 October 1990.
4 P. Agana, Training Day for Black Women – Working and Living With the Effects of Child Sexual Assault, London, 14 February 1990.
5 L. Armstrong, *Trouble and Strife*, No.21, Summer, 1991.
6 E. Driver, *Child Sexual Abuse: Feminist Perspectives*, Macmillan, London, 1990.
7 S. Francis, Personal interview, 2 May 1991.

Chapter 7

Remembering, coping, healing

1 C. Herron, Personal Interview, 21 May 1992.
2 L. Hollies, 'A Daughter Survives Incest', *Sage*, 4 (2), Fall 1987.
3 A. Lorde, *Sister, Outsider*, Crossing Press, Trumansburg N.Y., 1984.
4 Ibid., pp.166–7.
5 B.Y. Avery, of National Black Women's Health Project, USA, speaking in Cambridge, Massachusetts, July 1988.
6 D. Finkelhor, *Child Sexual Abuse: New Theory and Research*, The Free Press, New York, 1984.

INDEX

Melba Wilson was born in Virginia and raised in Texas. Based in London since 1977, she is a freelance journalist writing on health and social issues relating to Britain's black communities, with particular reference to black women.

Her articles, reviews and essays have been published in *New Society, Feminist Review, City Limits* and *Africa* magazine. She has contributed to several anthologies including *Why Children?* (The Women's Press, 1980), *Charting the Journey: Writing by Black and Third World Women* (Sheba Feminist Publishers, 1987) and *Feminism and Censorship* (Prism Press, 1988). She is the editor of *Healthy and Wise: The Essential Health Handbook for Black Women* (Virago, 1994).

SELECTED TITLES FROM SEAL PRESS